MediCaring Communities

MEDICARING COMMUNITIES

*Getting What We Want and Need in Frail Old Age
At an Affordable Cost*

*By Joanne Lynn, MD
and The Center for Elder Care and Advanced Illness
Altarum Institute*

Book design by Les Morgan.

Createspace First Edition (June 2016)
ISBN-13: 978-1481266918
ISBN-10: 1481266918

"You never change things by fighting the existing reality. To change something, build a new model that makes the existing model obsolete."

—*Buckminster Fuller*

Contents

Preface

This initiative and book owe much to many contributors and well-wishers. I am grateful to those who tested some of the elements, provided ideas, and supported the cause. Altarum Institute's Center for Elder Care and Advanced Illness generated the team that worked so hard to get the details right, and that team includes Elizabeth Blair, Jade Gong, Jim Lee, Anne Montgomery, Les Morgan, Judith Peres, and Holly Stanley. Altarum's President and CEO, Lincoln Smith, and its Board of Trustees have been stalwart and encouraging supporters. The Milbank Foundation and The Lawrence & Rebecca Stern Family Foundation provided critically important funding. The Retirement Research Foundation funded some of our work on care planning. Many colleagues have read and commented on various facts and proposals, and we hope that many more will help polish and test the proposals. This book is being self-published on the internet and in hard copy so that it is easy to improve as we all learn more. Please go to *medicaring.org* to join in the commentary. Together we can build on the opportunity to have what we most need and want in our futures as old people.

We have published some of this material in professional journals, aiming to spread the concepts and engender advice and criticism.[1,2] We have registered the trademark "MediCaring®" in order to protect it from commercial use by others and thus to have it available to mark this reform agenda. We do not otherwise intend to restrict the use of the term.

---

[1] (Lynn and Montgomery 2015)
[2] (Montgomery and Lynn 2014)

Introduction

Have you taken care of your mother or father as they lived out the last years of long lives? Or seen what happens to a friend's parents, or someone else you knew and loved, who grew to be very old? Listen to how we talk about the experience. Mostly, we'll experience travail, high costs, uncertainty, anxiety, frustration, and a generally difficult set of experiences. But sometimes things will go well—and the family caregivers and friends left behind will say, "Weren't we lucky!" and go on to attribute the good luck to some specific happenstance. "My sister is a hospice nurse," or "Our doctor was terrific," or "Mom had the good sense to move into assisted housing and later to turn down most everything that the doctors suggested." The reforms that this book presents—MediCaring Communities—aim to make it routine to get reliable and effective services, so that no one has to be lucky in order to have what they most need and want in old age. Let's re-engineer the service delivery system to meet the needs we will have when old, at a cost that families and the society can afford!

Getting elder care right has never been more important. Just a few generations ago, people rarely survived into frail old age, and very few physicians thought that elders should be subjected to surgical operations or any other troublesome medical interventions. Most people still lived on farms, where there was usually room to take in a relative, and someone in the extended family was able to be nearby most of the time. For millions of Americans, their family members are now widely scattered, working full-time, or otherwise unavailable. Everything has changed, except for the love and concern of family members and friends. Most Americans now will live into advanced old age, usually with multiple chronic conditions, disabilities, and fragile health. For people alive at age 65, the average man can now expect 1.5 years and the average woman, 2.5 years, of needing someone's help every day for "activities of daily living" like eating, toileting, moving about, and getting dressed.[3] But in most cases, our children can no longer take extended periods of time away from work to provide extensive direct supportive care, in part because they lack adequate retirement security for themselves. Many are also old enough to have some limitations themselves. A 95-year old mother may not be able to get much help from her two 70-something surviving children, both of whom are working part-time while dealing with their own arthritis and heart disease.

We forget that when Medicare started, 50 years ago, the average age at death was just 70 years old.[4] Now we get another decade, and that matters in many ways. The numbers are just starting to reshape the social order. Much more fundamental change is coming. Frail elders were rare in 1965 when Medicare started. Using age as a marker for frailty, the number of people 85 years old and older in the U.S. in 1960 was just under 1 million.[5] By 2000, we had 4.2 million.[6] By 2050, we'll have 18 million.[7] People over 85 constitute the most rapidly growing part of the American population. Between 2010 and 2050, the under-15 population is projected to increase by only 17% while the number of people over 85 will increase by 231%.[8,9]

We have done very little to prepare for this aging population. The current "care system" developed around a different set of perspectives and demographic imperatives and it seriously fails to serve the needs and priorities of the frail elderly population now. Too many elders are hospitalized because we have no services standing ready to support them at home, or they have to move to nursing homes because we fail

---

[3] (Favreault and Dey 2015)

[4] (United States Census Bureau 2003)

[5] (West, et al. 2014)

[6] (West, et al. 2014)

[7] (Ortman, Velkoff and Hogan 2014)

[8] (Pew Research Center 2014)

[9] (Administration on Aging, Administration for Community Living, Projected Future Growth of the Older Population 2005)

to make adapted and supported housing available. Elders routinely take inappropriate medications, suffer adverse events from errors in medications, are subjected to ill-advised tests, and undergo inappropriate treatments because the culture and the health care system fail to recognize that it is different to be living with serious progressive disability in old age than it is to be younger, with more resilience and more lifetime ahead. This mismanagement inflicts suffering on frail elderly people, uses up their savings, and wears out their family members.

Elders and their families deserve better—and we will deserve better in our own old age. But we will only achieve good care for frail elders if we learn how to stop the suffering, stop the waste, and stop the pretense that somehow just one more drug or medical breakthrough will make it all better and stave off death. In fact, what will make the lives of old people better is a thoughtfully arranged system that provides appropriate services at an affordable cost to them and society. Unlike some of the very difficult economic and environmental issues that face the country, a good plan is easy to find for the predictable rise in frail elders—that good plan is in this book! What we lack is only the energy and imagination to make it happen. That's what this book hopes to change.

Signals of a willingness to undergo reform are beginning to appear. After decades of functioning as an insurance plan, Medicare has become an active participant in change, offering tests of new models and more aligned incentives at a remarkable rate. Academics and philanthropies now push for addressing problems with the social determinants of health and lament our society's use of health care as an inadequate remedy for shortcomings in housing, food, jobs, and other constituents of good health. Financing of long-term care has come back to the policymaker agenda after a long hiatus.[10,11,12] The stage is set for serious and enduring reforms.[13]

---

[10] (Favreault, Gleckman and Johnson 2015)

This book proposes a thoroughly pragmatic plan—*MediCaring Communities*. The MediCaring reform process has six core components that fit together like the disparate elements of a machine that produces a good product only when all the parts work together. The following chapters will fill in the details and lay out a strategy for how to get from the here and now, with a care system that is indefensible and costly, to a future that bodes well for our ever-more diverse, multi-generational society.

The most dramatic changes from present practices are twofold. *First*, each frail elderly person has a unique set of hopes, priorities, strengths, personal resources, and medical conditions. Each person therefore needs a customized plan of services, not just the standard medical treatment for each malady. *Second*, support for each frail elderly person is anchored in his or her local community. Communities should play an important role in helping to plan and integrate the wide variety of services that elders need to stay out of crisis, and in co-managing improvement activities and funding priorities. At first, our proposed reforms may seem to be too difficult to engineer, but multiple strategies can work well, starting with the advantages some communities have because they have strong Programs of All-Inclusive Care for the Elderly, called "PACE."

---

[11] (Hayes, et al. 2016)
[12] (LeadingAge 2016)
[13] (Lynn and Blair 2016)

Core Components of a MediCaring Community

1. Frail elders identified in a geographic community

2. Longitudinal, comprehensive, elder-driven care plans

3. Medical care tailored to frail elders

4. Scope to include social and supportive services

5. Monitoring and improvement by a Community Board

6. Financing with savings from Medicare

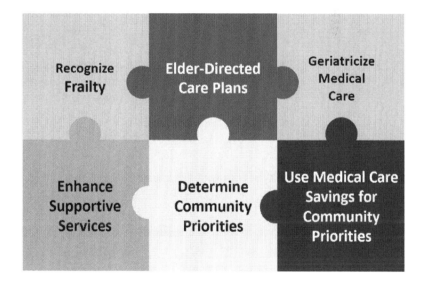

Core Component #1: Frail Elders Identified in a Geographic Community

The first key element of the MediCaring Communities service delivery reform is to develop a focus on frail elders—to recognize this newly common phase of life and to see that it has characteristic joys and troubles and also requires different social arrangements than those that served us earlier in life, even different from earlier in retirement age.

This sounds so straightforward, but that awareness is difficult to achieve, because simply acknowledging this phase of life is so new for our culture. Our cultural myth is that people live mostly healthy until they either die suddenly or contract a "serious" illness which turns into a "terminal" illness, following a course like Figure 1.1.

Figure 1.1: Classic "Terminal" Disease: "Dying"

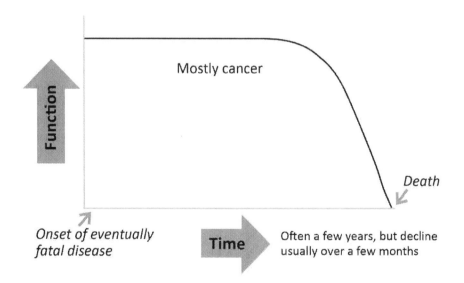

However, now most of us will have a "frailty" course, much more like Figure 1.2, in which there is no clear "terminal" phase and the "dying" can be cut short by, for example, a pneumonia or a stroke, or the person can continue for remarkable lengths of time with increasingly severe limitations.

Figure 1.2: Prolonged Dwindling

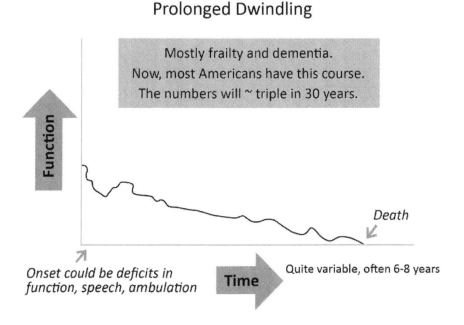

We have no popular stories about living through this part of life—no heroes, no villains, simply nothing useful. Elderly people searching for a reference point sometimes voice a strong preference not to live in a permanently unconscious status like the court cases of Ms. Theresa Shiavo or Ms. Karen Ann Quinlan, though the elderly person has no real likelihood of experiencing that outcome. Very few stories are well enough known to use as a benchmark. We know almost nothing of Ronald Reagan with dementia and what he and his caregivers went through. We have almost no movies or TV dramas (or comedies!) about this part of life. So, we have the remarkable opportunity, and the obligation, to create our myths and standards anew, and to be thoughtful about the stories we teach our children to admire. Indeed, once we recognize this nearly new phase of life, we can define its meaning in our lives. But the fact that the society has not yet built our stories and myths makes it difficult for people to identify the frail phase of life or to realize that it is very different to feel the limitations of chronic conditions in old age than to be ill when younger.

The language to use in dealing with policy and practice concerning frail elders deserves brief mention, and the reader will find a useful Glossary in the back of the book. This book will mostly use the term *frail elders* to refer to elderly people living with fragile health due to multiple chronic conditions and progressive disabilities. Some common terms tend to diminish the richness and humanity of frail elders. For example, *elders* are only *patients* or *clients* when in certain relationships. This category of frail elders includes elderly persons affected by serious illnesses or disabilities, including old age itself, that tend to worsen over time, greatly diminish resilience to stress, and require ongoing help from other people. This chapter will provide more details about defining the category.

Various professionals such as nurse practitioners and physician assistants have medical duties that overlap the role of the physician, but for simplicity, we will call them all *physicians*. Likewise, we will use *family* to include all those who are emotionally bonded to the frail elderly person, whether by friendship, relationship, or law, so *family caregiver* includes the long-term friend who provides personal care and coordination, just as a relative might. The diversity of our society requires that social policies be very inclusive and supportive of all who would help frail elders. LTSS stands for Long-Term Services and Supports. LTSS includes all the non-medical elements that go into supporting a frail elder across time, such as assistance with bathing and dressing and help buying and preparing food.

Finally, frail elderly people and their families have noticed that this is the last phase of life, and that the outcome is death, and they usually want to have this weigh in the decision-making and to be acknowledged. But our culture has only the language of "end of life," "terminal disease," and "ready for hospice." These phrases do not usefully describe persons with persistently uncertain timing of death. So, we will work with longer phrases and helpful honesty, and the reader can try out language and phrasing that is supportive, kind, and honest.

This chapter responds to these key questions:

1. Who is frail and what characterizes that experience?

2. How do people transition into frailty?

3. Why organize services for frail people by geographic community?

4. Why refer frail elders to a MediCaring service delivery system?

5. How could a community system find and offer MediCaring to frail elderly people?

1.1 Who is frail and what characterizes that experience?

Oliver Wendell Holmes wrote of a "wonderful one-hoss shay" that was built so well that no part could break down ahead of the others. Rather, after one hundred years, "it all went to pieces all at once,—All at once and nothing first,—Just as bubbles do when they burst."[14] Once, the commonplace way to come to the end of life was for something to break down in our bodies—injuries, heart attacks, infections, childbirth complications, cancers, and all the ordinary "causes of death." Better health and health care has made these much less common, and more and more of us now get the opportunity to live into old age. However, we won't quite end as the one-hoss shay did, with good health until the day that everything falls apart. Instead, we will have diminished reserve in many parts of our bodies and some parts which are really not functioning well but which are supported by some medication or treatment that keeps us going, until finally enough goes wrong that life ends. Basically, frailty is that period of living with the disabilities, chronic conditions, and diminished reserves associated with aging.

What is the experience of this part of life? As with most of life, experience varies. All too many people live with pain and other adverse symptoms and confront a health care system that is often frustrating, unreliable, and error-prone. Many elders also have financial problems, leading to compromising on food, housing, and medicines, and often to an unnecessarily early isolation from social groups and friends. However, many people also find remarkable opportunities for fulfillment and joy. This can be a time for reflecting on a life well-lived or fully atoned for, a time of completion and celebration of life's projects, contemplation of life's meaning, or for sharing insights from experience. In short, one hopes that the time before the end of life is meaningful, comfortable, and comforting, despite infirmities and losses.

---

[14] (Holmes 2009)

Having most people achieve these goals, however, faces considerable challenges. Our everyday social arrangements have not planned for a large population with progressive and severe disabilities. Examples range from the lack of grab bars in bathrooms to the lack of arrangements for family members and other volunteers to provide support without losing their jobs. In addition, the culture is beset with pervasive ageism that counts old people with disabilities as embarrassing, burdensome, invisible, or worse. Many elders will have cognitive failure as a major part of their frailty course. One estimate is that between 18% and 38% of people living past 85 years old and between 28% and 44% of those 90 and older have significant cognitive failure.[15] Living with dementia and other brain malfunctions poses challenges for meaningfulness and comfort for the affected individuals and substantial burdens for their family caregivers. The financial costs and the social meanings of caregiving and other support for persons living with dementia pose challenges that the culture has not yet confronted.

What is it that frail elders most want? The best answer to this is always, "Ask the elder." People become more and more differentiated from others over their lifetimes. Each of us arrives at old age with one-of-a-kind history, personal relationships, resources, and, most important, goals and priorities for the rest of life. An elderly person still responsible for a developmentally disabled son will often feel very protective of finances to assure that person's future, while a similarly ill elderly person may have no one for whom to save money. One person can focus on eternity and salvation, while his neighbor has no religious inclination.

However, frail elderly people do have some priorities and concerns that are generally held, and that are substantially different from our priorities earlier in life. A mature realism about the limitations of medical care usually leads to abandoning illusions of cure and accommodating various disabilities and ongoing medical attention.

---

[15] (Gardner, Valcour and Yaffe 2013)

As daily life becomes more challenging, having competent and compatible supportive assistance (by family, friends, or paid attendants) becomes newly important, along with having trustworthy professional advice on medical and financial matters. Reliability matters more and more—having the feeling that one is well-prepared and also has good back-up for unplanned changes in health or living arrangements. Most elders very much want to stay as independent as possible as long as possible. Most who still have any tangible assets would like to avoid impoverishment and possibly to leave a financial legacy for family or charity. Many worry about the changes in the lives of family members that caregiving entails, and they wish to avoid the isolation for patient and caregiver that often accompanies mobility problems, memory problems, and family caregiving. Frail elders are also acquainted with the fact of dying and ordinarily wish to make decisions that reflect an awareness of the limited time left; indeed, they often find it odd that physicians and family members dodge this obvious fact.[16] These considerations are generally muted earlier in life, when what one wanted from health care was mostly restoration of health, or prevention of health problems. So long as health could be restored, pursuing that possibility mostly overwhelmed everything else. The priorities and concerns of frail elders are different, and often are more complex and personal.

Widely available medical care has both helped to create the opportunity to grow old and has complicated pursuit of the goals of meaningfulness and comfort. Medical care in the U.S. has been quite aggressive in offering procedures, costly medications, and other treatments. While these have often been beneficial, sometimes they were not desired and might have been actually harmful to the frail elderly person.[17]

---

[16] (Ahalt, et al. 2012)
[17] (American Geriatrics Society Choosing Wisely Workgroup 2013)

Where are the gaps? Medicare in the U.S. does not generally pay for care of teeth, hearing, eyesight, nutrition, feet, or mobility, all of which are centrally important to frail elderly people. Medicare also does not generally provide for personal care such as giving a bath or providing food with a spoon, nor does it provide support for a family caregiver. Elderly people and their families have to sort out how to get these other services and to manage and pay for them, until they are poor enough to get whatever services that their state provides through Medicaid. Some services are intended for broad support of all frail elders under federal initiatives (e.g., Meals on Wheels under the Older Americans Act) or state or local support, but these are routinely overbooked and appropriations for them are declining in the face of increasing demand.[18]

The services frail elders most need are hard to find, hard to pay for, hard to coordinate, difficult to evaluate, and generally frustrating— so they often are simply not provided. Various layers of coordinators, navigators, and managers have arisen to patch these problems, but their effectiveness is limited by the underlying chaos of a "system" that has no intrinsic coordination or management and that had developed to serve a very different, younger and less disabled, population.

The number of Americans over 85 will more than triple, from 5.8 million in 2012 to 18 million in 2050.[19] Quite simply, a phase of life that almost did not exist a century ago is now expectable: most of us will live to become old and frail before we die, and social arrangements have not caught up. We have all sorts of arrangements to accommodate raising children, from marriage to public schools, but we have had children to raise throughout history. Now we have a new phase of life, and we need to develop useful patterns, quickly.

---

[18] (United States Government Accountability Office, Older Americans Act: Updated Information on Unmet Need for Services 2015)
[19] (Ortman, Velkoff and Hogan 2014)

1.2 How do people transition into frailty?

While the background decline in the reserve capacity of a person's various bodily functions is gradual, the onset of the experience of frailty can be sudden, for example, arising from a serious stroke or a crippling heart attack. Most people, however, gradually accumulate chronic conditions and the sum of their effects is what begins to erode the person's ability to function in daily activities. For example, the person living with emphysema in her 80's begins to find it difficult to take a bath, at least on bad days. Or a person with mild dementia begins to get lost in the neighborhood. Some people have no particular medical illness, but just gradually slow down, lose weight, become weaker and feel tired.

Events that were once minor annoyances will throw a frail person off course: One bad fall, and the injuries and fear make it impossible for the person to live alone again. With a little more loss of sight, an elderly person cannot drive to get food or to visit friends. The margin between living as we wish and being in serious trouble becomes quite thin. Physiologically, people in their eighties and beyond usually have very little reserve in most organ systems, so a challenge to the heart, or lungs, or kidneys, or any other organ system leads to evident and serious illness.

The fact that most of us have no clear onset of frailty mirrors our maturing from children into adults. While social conventions call for certain attributes of adulthood to be assumed at various ages, from about 16 to 21 years old, actually becoming reasonably mature adults is a gradual process. We don't yet have the social conventions for marking frailty's onset, in part because the transitions are usually so gradual and the benefits of noticing have been minimal. Under a MediCaring Community model, a frail elderly person will benefit from having a service delivery system that optimizes his or her well-being, so early work on MediCaring Communities will need to develop some conventions on boundaries and expectations. We propose some candidate criteria in section 1.5 (page 18).

1.3 Why organize services for frail people by geographic community?

One of the most characteristic aspects of the frail period of life is that the person becomes quite tied to home and community. This is not a time when people travel far away on adventures, or even undertake travel for medical consultation. The range of moving around becomes smaller, and the services the person needs, such as home-delivered meals and personal care, are mostly tied to where he or she lives. Eventually, going out to see a doctor becomes a major production, requiring help from family and specially equipped transportation, so many frail elders come to see physicians only in the emergency room or in a hospital or nursing home. Senator Rockefeller once told the painful story of trying to get suitable help for his mother, living with dementia. His bottom line and ours is that even having money and influence cannot guarantee getting suitable support at home if the community has no trained workforce.

Remarkable efficiencies become possible in organizing care geographically, once many services need to happen where frail elders live. Now, we send a dozen aides from half a dozen companies into an apartment building where six people live who need a couple of hours of services in the morning and evening. Instead, a geographically organized service could send in half as many aides, pay them better, have them move around as different people need them in the building, give better care, and still come out costing much less. Similarly, if a dozen frail elders live down one road, sending a dozen different physicians or nurses out to see them entails a great deal of "windshield time," which would be better spent if one or two went out and attended to all who need the service along that road. In addition, a team working in one area gets to know a lot about subtle elements that make the work more efficient or effective: they learn which pharmacy will deliver after hours, which church will provide food in a difficult situation, which roads will close in bad weather, and the thousand other things that make local endeavors work well. Various rules defending the appearance of competition now prevent implementing this commonsense approach.

Having a strong community will protect the interests of current and future frail elders. Stakeholders include frail elders and family members, service providers, and ordinary citizens, all of whom are prone to pay attention to the quality and supply of all of the needed services. All who are aware of the interests of their community can play a role in influencing societal arrangements, setting priorities, and allocating the authority and accountability for effective and efficient services. Having frail elder care become, in part, a responsibility of the community will also help build communities, just as taking responsibility for roads, schools, and business growth does.

The need for reform is urgent. Continuing the current course is impossible. Every analysis of the economic effects of the predictable aging of the American population shows that, without reductions in per capita costs and changes in financing strategies, the combination of Social Security, Medicare, and Medicaid expenditures will be inadequate to meet the need while also being an unprecedented threat to the economy.[20] Hubert Humphrey's famous quote in the entry hall of the Health and Human Services building in Washington, DC, holds that "the moral test of government is how that government treats those who are in the dawn of life, the children; those who are in the twilight of life, the elderly; and those who are in the shadows of life, the sick, the needy and the handicapped." Both for good moral reasons and for our own self-protection, we do not want our governments to fail in providing for the elderly, but we cannot simply keep doing what we have been doing: current practices are too costly and provide inadequately for what we most need when old and frail. So, we need a plan that assures needed services at an affordable cost. At this time, in this country, allowing some willing communities to step ahead and teach the rest of us how to succeed is a politically acceptable way forward.

---

[20] (National Research Council 2012)

1.4 Why refer frail elders to a MediCaring service delivery system?

The question here is whether frail elderly people could just opt into MediCaring services from time to time and stay in some other payment and delivery system at other times. Two strong reasons argue against this course. First, the MediCaring approach is meant to be comprehensive, to build on a strong and shared individual care plan, and to be supportive of the elderly person (and family) goals at every turn. Having frail elders use whatever services happen to be offered at any point would eliminate the coherence and excellence of the overall plan and would make it very difficult to manage. This would invite the chaos that would ensue if every high school student could just drop into classes of interest, anywhere in the county. There would be no continuity, no overall plan to assure timeliness and adequate coverage, and no management of the system supply and quality. In addition, at least the first years of MediCaring depend upon capturing the savings from more prudent and appropriate use of Medicare-covered services. Calculating those savings is much more plausible for a well-defined population, even though it would always be possible to sign up and later leave the program. The elderly person keeps control.

1.5 How could a community system find and offer MediCaring to frail elderly people who would benefit?

This question requires attention to the specifics of how to define the population in a way that is practical, which ultimately requires working with the data that is actually available as communities start to implement MediCaring. The leading research definition of frailty is this: "A clinical syndrome in which three or more of the following criteria were present: unintentional weight loss (ten pounds in past year), self-reported exhaustion, weakness (grip strength), slow walking speed, and low physical activity."[21] An elderly person with none of the indicators is "robust," a person with one or two indicators is classified as "pre-frail," and a person with three or more indicators is "frail." This research definition is a welcome guidepost, but most of these elements are not in existing records, and a workable plan cannot require outreach in person to every older person to test the criteria for entry.

Furthermore, the MediCaring services should reach some elderly people who have not lost weight, strength or energy but who are already disabled from a major chronic condition or from a combination of multiple chronic conditions. Our definition of frailty includes disabilities and memory problems, so the scope is broader than the research definition. For example, a person living with the effects of a disabling stroke or moderate dementia might well have none of the research criteria, but the person would still be appropriate for a MediCaring Community initiative.

Once MediCaring becomes popular and well-known, people who are not yet frail, but who are quite old and realize that their next health challenge is likely to leave them more disabled and frail, might well want to be able to rely upon a care system that makes sense. This would parallel the commonplace practice of a woman who is hoping to become pregnant who establishes a relationship with an obstetrician-gynecologist ahead of time. In our frail elder population, a person at 90 years of age who realizes that her strength is declining and that her chronic emphysema is likely to pose complications during the coming winter might well want to join a coherent and sensible service delivery system tailored to her needs, even before actually becoming disabled.

To help establish some practical approaches, we undertook analyses of Medicare payments and data from the Health and Retirement Study, which interviews a nationally representative sample of people older than 55 and their principal personal representative,

---

[21] (Fried, et al. 2001)

every two years.[22] We tried out a criterion of having reported that the elderly person needed someone's help with two or more of the six activities of daily living (ADLs) that are commonly catalogued. We set the bar at two ADLs because that is usually the level that requires nearly constant attendance by another person who is able to help, and because that is a common criterion for state Medicaid programs to cover a nursing home level of care. About one-tenth of all those over age 65 reported this level of disability in any one interview cycle, and only about one-tenth of them ever reported an improved level of disability before dying. This criterion fits common sense and either is or readily could be available, even by over-the-phone interview. A few people have this sort of disability only transiently, as when they are recovering from surgery, and that could readily be determined. The cohort could also include elders who have sufficient dementia to have poor judgment and require nearly constant attendance by another person, while still being able to do ADLs independently. As mentioned above, making MediCaring available to elderly people who are not yet disabled is justified when that person wants a sensible care system and is at increasingly high risks from age and lack of reserves when any additional health problems arise. In sum, the inclusion criteria could be as follows.

---

[22] (Health and Retirement Study 2016)

Figure 1.3: Identification of Frail Elders in Need of MediCaring

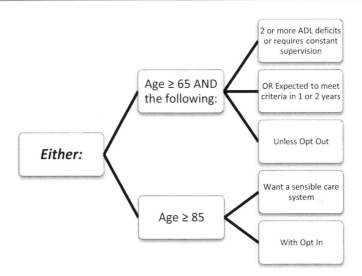

Of course, any particular community may have other data to use or priorities that justify different thresholds, so the first MediCaring Communities will need to adapt this initial set of criteria. In general, MediCaring Communities could start with people identified as they seek help in the medical care system. Most frail people now are in the hospital or the emergency room within any given year, so mining those records will yield the first set of potential MediCaring participants. One might be able to use the data gathered on admission to a nursing home (the Minimum Data Set [MDS]) or a home care agency (the Outcome and Assessment Information Set [OASIS] data) to find people needing help with two or more ADLs. The Welcome to Medicare exam and the Annual Wellness Visit are Medicare preventive care planning visits that are being more broadly implemented and could serve to find frail elders within physician practices. In many parts of the country, Meals on Wheels and similar nutrition programs require nearly this level of disability, so implementing outreach through senior nutrition, programs will identify another cohort. As the program spreads and stories appear in local news media and in community settings like churches and clubs, referrals from family, elderly people, and their neighbors will arise. The aim would be to make MediCaring available to all who prefer the MediCaring approach and are eligible within a defined geographic area. Until all areas have a MediCaring program, there will be calls to serve some in a fringe around the local geographic boundaries, and communities will have to decide whether and under what conditions to allow a somewhat variable border.

For a frail elderly person, initiating MediCaring services should be available at any time. The 72 year old person with a profound stroke or the 92 year old who has just witnessed a difficult course for a similarly aged neighbor are in the sort of situation that motivates signing up for MediCaring. They need to be able to join when motivated and when their condition qualifies them to do so, without waiting for the Medicare annual enrollment period or even until the start of the next month.

In the early years, before the MediCaring program has a strong track record and experience with outreach and retention, respect for the participants requires that they be able to leave and return to traditional Medicare or perhaps to their previous managed care plan at nearly any time. Once the MediCaring Community program is well established, the administrative burden of allowing quick shifts might prove to be unnecessary.

Core Component #2: Longitudinal, Comprehensive, Elder-driven Care Plans

Life gets complicated when you are old and frail. You are usually living on a fixed, and often fairly thin, income. You worry about whether your savings will last to the end of your life and whether those last days will be awful. You have to deal with losses in your capabilities and in your network of friends and family. You live with the constraints of various physical maladies. For people over 85 years old, 83% have two or more chronic conditions.[23] Most people over age 65 take more than five medications.[24] About one-third of people living past the age of 85 will develop dementia.[25] Many more have confusion or delirium when they have a bout of worsening illness or when taking a new medication. If you arrive at frail old age with attentive family or friends, they are part of the experience and their burdens and issues weigh on you. If you don't have family or friends, then you are often feeling quite alone and even wronged, without anyone on your side or caring about you. Housing that has served you well for years becomes unsafe or simply too expensive. Even getting food can be daunting. And yet it all has to work, every day, for you to live well—even when something goes wrong or your health and capabilities suffer a decline.

The most missing element in care for frail elders has to be a thoughtful, negotiated care plan. What we usually have instead is a set of diagnoses, medications and treatments that respond to some current symptoms or concerns, and perhaps an uncoordinated assortment of social and supportive services from different sources—none of which reflects a consideration of the priorities and possibilities for this elderly person and his or her family. A good care plan, in contrast, articulates the actions needed in order for the frail elder to live well, with priorities and goals determined by the elderly person and his or her

---

[23] (Centers for Medicare and Medicaid Services, Chronic Conditions Among Medicare Beneficiaries 2012)
[24] (Qato, et al. 2016)
[25] (Gardner, Valcour and Yaffe 2013)

family. The plan is created by the care team, consisting of the most important service providers along with the patient and family. A thorough care plan deals with the more likely and the more problematic contingencies. It is also honest about what the elder and the family can expect in the future and about what choices they really have.

Most medical records don't even have a space for writing down a care plan or the members of the care team. Most don't even identify the primary caregiver in the home. Even when care plans exist, key service providers or the elderly person and family often have not participated in formulating them or have access to them when needed. Yet, planning ahead is the heart of good care for living with chronic conditions.

Generating a good care plan is like many other complex planning activities. It goes substantially beyond just reacting to current events or addressing a narrow scope of concerns. Like a comprehensive plan for urban development or for training an athlete, a worthy care plan builds on an honest understanding of the current situation and how it could unfold with various actions and events. The care plan articulates the goals and values of the frail elderly person and the family and crafts a set of actions to achieve the best available outcome, as judged from the perspective of the elderly person and his or her family. Thinking through the most important issues and coming to decisions and plans can enable the frail elder to live well, as he or she (with family) defines "living well."

In the last few years, many endeavors have underlined the central role of care plans. Some Accountable Care Organizations are beginning to measure care plan development along with Annual Wellness Exams. The 2014 Institute of Medicine (IOM) report on end of life care makes care planning a central concern in the time of living with serious illness ahead of death.[26] Most of the integrated care demonstrations for dual eligible (eligible for both Medicare and

---

[26] (Institute of Medicine 2014)

Medicaid) beneficiaries in certain states are requiring care planning for complex patients. PACE, skilled nursing facilities (SNFs), and hospice programs already do care planning, though hospices generally focus just on comfort and supportive services and SNFs generally focus on rehabilitation.

More recently, the 2015 CMS Measure Applications Partnership report, "Cross-Cutting Challenges Facing Measurement" identified a number of gaps in the measurement of care plans, emphasizing the need for person-centered care plans created early in the care process, with identified goals, and "social care planning addressing social, practical, and legal needs of patient and caregivers."[27] The American Geriatrics Society also cited "an individualized, goal-oriented care plan based on the person's preferences" as an essential element of person-centered care.[28] The 2015 proposed rule for Meaningful Use Stage 3 (governing the requirements for electronic medical records) recommended the inclusion of a certification criterion for care plans that would allow "a user to record, change, access, create and receive care plan information."[29] In the final regulation for the chronic care management (CCM) code, Medicare required the maintenance of an electronic care plan as one of five capabilities necessary to bill with the CCM codes.[30] A recent Medicare notice of proposed rulemaking for the Requirements for Long-Term Care Facilities adds a new "Comprehensive Person-Centered Care Planning" section, which would require facilities to take the resident's goals and preferences into consideration in developing the care plan.[31] One unique aspect of the new requirements is the inclusion of the full interdisciplinary team

---

[27] (National Quality Forum 2015)
[28] (American Geriatrics Society Expert Panel on Person-Centered Care 2015)
[29] (Office of the National Coordinator for Health Information Technology, Meaningful Use Stage 3, 80 FR 62648 2015)
[30] (Centers for Medicare and Medicaid Services, Chronic Care Management Regulation, 79 FR 67715 2014)
[31] (Centers for Medicare and Medicaid Services, 80 FR 42168 2015)

(IDT) in the care planning, including direct care staff such as nurse's aides. The Care Planning Act of 2015, introduced by Senator Mark Warner and others, would require Medicare to cover advanced illness planning and coordination services for eligible individuals.[32] These services would include "Assisting the individual in defining and articulating goals of care, values, and preferences" and discussing a range of treatment options.

With so many parties championing care planning, the slow uptake is perplexing. Currently, most people will go through their period of frailty without ever having a comprehensive, person-centered care plan. At least for frail elders, improving this situation is critically important and reliable, effective, comprehensive care planning has to be a core achievement of a MediCaring Community.

This chapter responds to these key questions:

2.1 What processes are essential in generating good care plans?

2.2 How could the delivery system evaluate and improve the care planning process?

2.3 How could the delivery system use care plans to improve the service supply and quality?

---

[32] (The Care Planning Act of 2015, S.1549 2015)

2.1 What processes are essential in generating good care plans?

Developing a good care plan, and doing it efficiently and effectively for a great many complicated situations, is difficult. Perhaps that is why we have no examples of good care planning processes brought to scale for a sizable population of frail elders. Of course, barriers also arise from having no reimbursement tied to comprehensive care planning and having most of the key members of the care team dispersed geographically with no personal relationship with one another. These conditions are exactly what need to change. Without a good care plan being created and implemented, the elderly person is constantly caught in a reactive mode of responses to whatever calamities arise and constant anxiety. In contrast, a good care plan ensures thoughtful preparation to support the person through likely situations. Having many people with good care plans in a community will ensure that services come to be organized to deliver on whatever is most important to frail elderly persons and their families. The consequences of the gaps between current dysfunctions and good care practices are often starkly clear. For example:

- A frail elder with a good care plan will have a back-up plan in case a family caregiver becomes ill; a frail elder in the usual care system will be transported to the emergency room when the caregiver is suddenly unavailable.

- A frail elder with a good care plan peaceably dies at home and loved ones are present or notified; a frail elder in the usual care gets a painful and expensive assault by well-meaning emergency responders who have no choice but to try resuscitation and rescue.

A good care plan must address expected situations requiring rapid decision making, such as appropriate response to cardiac arrest and death, and must deal with recurrent problematic treatment issues, such as hospitalization or artificial nutrition. But care plans are not just for medical treatments. They also honor personally meaningful relationships and activities, document trade-offs between medical treatment and life enjoyment, and build on the availability and skills of family and other caregivers. The care plan must move with the patient across settings and time, be revised as situations change and at planned intervals, and be evaluated for achievement of goals. Evaluations of the care planning process and the care plans should be reported to service providers involved in the planning, so their work can improve.

A set of voluntary committees sponsored by the Office of the National Coordinator for Health Information Technology recently has been working to build care plans into health records. Figure 2.1 is their summary graphic concerning care plans helps to anchor the MediCaring approach to care plans.[33]

Medicare proposed a reasonable suggested list of care plan elements in their regulation establishing the CCM payment code.[34] This includes:

- A problem list,
- Expected outcome and prognosis,
- Measurable treatment goals,
- Symptom management and planned interventions,
- Medication management,
- Community/social services to be accessed,
- Plan for care coordination with other providers,
- Responsible individual for each intervention, and
- Requirements for periodic review/revision.

A list like this probably seems so obvious that the usual patient assumes that it is in effect, and the complexities in the graphic might make the exercise appear daunting. However, complicated situations require solutions that do not oversimplify. Frail elders and their families deserve to expect that their care team functions as a team,

---

[33] (Garber, L and the S & I Framework 2014)
[34] (Centers for Medicare and Medicaid Services, Chronic Care Management Regulation, 79 FR 67715 2014)

thinks clearly about the future, makes useful recommendations, and respects the elderly person's priorities. The challenge is to build a delivery system that can regularly, efficiently, and competently deliver on that vision.

Figure 2.1: Care Plan Diagram

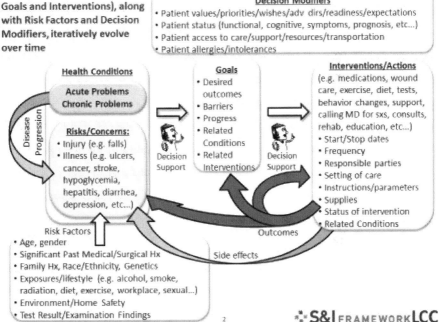

2.1.1 Understanding the frail elder's situation

The foundation of the care planning process lies in understanding the elderly person's situation well enough to build a practical and customized plan. Sometimes, a short-term plan has to spring from partial information, as when a person is brought to the emergency room without past records or a suitable informant. Often, the clinical team providing services has to balance the elderly person's interests in maintaining some zones of privacy and control with the likely importance of information gaps. But most often, the service providers simply do not ask about much of anything beyond issues of immediate importance in their own field of expertise. That is how elderly people who cannot climb stairs after hospital discharge are left at the curb by taxis, unable to get into their homes, or how elders who cannot cook or get food return to the hospital with dehydration after a few days at home. And that is how the elderly person and the family are left frustrated that no one has leveled with them as to how the situation is likely to evolve, while the elder and family make plans that do not work out because their expert advisors are not being accurate or helpful.

What domains are important for the clinical participants in the care team to understand in order to help the elderly person and family build a good care plan?

- Capacity of the elderly person to understand the situation and make his or her own decisions, and suitability and availability of an appropriate surrogate when needed (e.g., a person designated in a durable power of attorney or a close family member)[35]
- Medical status, current treatments, and the elderly person's likely course with each of various potentially attractive treatment and support options
- Functional status (e.g., Instrumental Activities of Daily Living (IADLs) and Activities of Daily Living (ADLs) and likely future function with the various options
- Financial and other resources needed for various plans of care and their availability
- Current living arrangements and how well they are working, including safety, affordability, and social interaction

---

[35] (The Commission on Law and Aging, American Bar Association 2011)

- Family/friend relationships that are important to the person or that might open options
- Access to appropriate food and a way to prepare and consume it
- Transportation, suitable for existing and likely future disabilities, including reliability and affordability
- Caregiver(s) identities, contact information, responsibilities, willingness, capabilities, and needs
- The language, culture, and personal stories that are meaningful to this elderly person and family, including religion and spirituality
- Decisions already made or needing to be made concerning future treatment and support, including preferences about the course near death (advance care planning),
- What matters most to the frail elder (and family): goals, preferences, and values

Much of this information can be obtained on a written survey that the elderly person or a knowledgeable caregiver can complete on their own time. Some information can come from medical or service provider records. However, often some of the important elements of the current situation requires skilled interviewing of and conversation with the elderly person and family. The inquiry usually is most productive when shaped by predictions of the likely future courses by the physician and the care team.

Many tools have arisen for establishing the baseline assessment, including the OASIS record required of Medicare home health providers and the MDS record required of all nursing home providers.[36,37] Some states have fielded their own forms as part of

---

[36] (Centers for Medicare and Medicaid Services, Outcome and Assessment Information Set (OASIS) 2012)

[37] (Centers for Medicare and Medicaid Services, MDS 3.0 RAI Manual 2016)

waiver programs, such as the MNChoice on-line instrument for Minnesota.[38] The new IMPACT statute will require standardization of a health assessment done by any skilled nursing facility, home health agency, inpatient rehabilitation facility, or long-term acute care hospital that serves a Medicare patient in the 90-day period after hospitalization.[39] Taking full effect by 2019, assessments required by IMPACT could follow the model of the CARE instrument, which serves as the framework for MDS (nursing homes) and OASIS (home care).[40] These standard data collection tools will be helpful in comparing outcomes and communicating among service providers. Supplementary information in narrative form will fill in a more complete understanding of the person's situation, his or her hopes and fears, and the likely outcomes.

One key component of good care planning is to assure that the relevant people who make up the care team can come to understand the situation and generate the plan. First among these people is the elder (to the degree he or she is capable), the family (if available), and anyone else important to decision-making and implementation of the plan from the elder's perspective. These key people are essential to the team and no plan can really go forward without their agreement. Current parlance is "patient-centered care plan," but that phrase does not put the elder in a strong position. One might instead phrase the product as an "elder-driven care plan."

Ordinarily, a physician or nurse practitioner needs to be on the team in order to provide prognostic information and to offer medical diagnoses and treatments. Usually, the team needs someone with skills in creatively matching needs with services and someone to help frail elders and families to feel confident and capable in managing everyday issues such as medications, appointments, personal care, nutrition, and

[38] (Minnesota Department of Human Services 2016)
[39] (Improving Medicare Post-Acute Transformation Act of 2014, Public Law 113-185 2014)
[40] (Centers for Medicare and Medicaid Services, CARE Item Set and B-CARE 2015)

engagement with health care and other service providers.[41] People with other special skills may need to be on the team for a particular elderly person: therapists to address particular rehabilitation possibilities, a consulting pharmacist to guide medication management, a mental health practitioner to help with serious behavior or mood problems, a wound care nurse to address a surgical or pressure wound, and so on. Usually, people who merely deliver something to the home are included in the plan but not on the team that develops the plan. Indeed, they usually do not have access to the plan. That can be an unfortunate omission. A person who delivers meals or oxygen, for example, can be a key observer to detect early signs that things are not going well. Their input could be part of the planning. Obviously, some situations require language translators, multiple conversations to assure understanding, awareness of and enhancement of health literacy, affirmative steps to overcome perceived or actual biases, and other elements of any complicated human undertaking.

Sometimes, the team is ongoing and at least the core participants, other than the elder and family, work together often, addressing multiple frail elderly people and their plans. Sometimes, instead, the team forms around a particular frail elder's challenges. Often, a few people are frequently involved and know one another well, and others are brought in when needed.

Teamwork is challenging, and teams ordinarily need training to be optimally effective. TeamSTEPPS is one popular and evidence-based training program.[42] The Geriatric Interdisciplinary Team Training from the Hartford Institute for Geriatric Nursing is another.[43] At the least, the service provider participants need to be able to communicate effectively with elders and family members, to enable all team members (including the elder and family members) to participate, to

---

[41] (Care Transitions Intervention n.d.)

[42] (Agency for Healthcare Research and Quality, TeamSTEPPS®: Strategies and Tools to Enhance Performance and Patient Safety n.d.)

[43] (Hartford Institute for Geriatric Nursing 2016)

bring reliable information to bear, to prioritize issues, to negotiate decisions, to take responsibility, and to document the plan. Following up to learn from implementation of care plans marks an unusually effective learning organization, since most care teams do little follow up or improvement activity.

2.1.2 Coming to accord on goals and services

Care planning starts with the frail elderly person's direct involvement as possible, or with a suitable surrogate speaking on the elderly person's behalf otherwise. Family caregivers and long-term paid caregivers usually should participate in designing and implementing the care plan, unless the elderly person objects or a caregiver has not yet been identified. The elderly person's priorities, treatment preferences, concerns, and future goals should anchor the care planning process. Information from clinical and social assessments, a list of medical diagnoses, and perspectives on the most likely course and the options for services that might affect the course often help to shape and sharpen the elderly person's priorities. The care team is charged with ensuring that potentially attractive options for support or treatment are offered and explored, including those that focus on supportive services and those that entail substantial medical intervention.

The options presented should have a real chance of being beneficial to the patient. Medical interventions that offer no benefit should not be mentioned, unless the patient or a family member asks about them. More problematic is the wide array of medical services that are often used but which offer very little benefit and, often, create the possibility of adverse effects or incidental findings that will cause further testing, treatment, and costs.[44] In a MediCaring Community, the medical clinicians should confer with affected elders, family members, and other clinicians in order to develop shared understandings of the merits of burdening patients and families with information about low-value (and possibly harmful) medical

---

[44] (Choosing Wisely 2016)

interventions like these. Some, like cardio-pulmonary resuscitation, might be widely misunderstood and merit discussion with each elderly person and family. Successful resuscitation is exceedingly unlikely and harms from the effort are obvious.[45] Other overuse situations, like multiple imaging studies for straightforward diagnoses, have grown up in an environment in which the patient and the physician have not needed to attend to costs, so any putative chance of benefit seemed adequate to justify use.[46,47]

The MediCaring Communities model will not bar access to any medical services covered under Medicare (or Medicaid). However, frail elders and families will choose to undertake some costly and burdensome medical treatments much less often when they are informed and engaged.[48,49] Rather than making any medical test or treatment unavailable, the MediCaring approach aims to ensure that frail elders and family members clearly understand just how much—or how little—certain procedures would be likely to offer. In this way, elderly persons will not find themselves barred from medical treatments that they understand and want. Rather, elders and their families would be part of the decision-making process and would be enabled to understand and decide which treatments really serve them best. If a frail elderly person is now 80% likely to get a test or treatment that is of dubious value, better counseling and care planning might well reduce that rate to 20%. So, a person who needs one imaging study will not end up having three, and an elderly person who does not stand to benefit will not be channeled into having an overwhelmingly burdensome operation that is appropriately routine and quickly healed for younger people.

---

[45] (Murphy, et al. 1994)
[46] (Shen, et al. 2004)
[47] (Berenson and Docteur 2013)
[48] (Cassel and Guest 2012)
[49] (Phillips, et al. 1996)

Articulating goals and preferences turns out to be an underdeveloped art form. Some physicians just ask whether the person is more invested in a long life or a comfortable one, and therefore whether the person is willing to forgo life-sustaining interventions in what would otherwise be an emergency effort at rescue. This is important, of course, and is the set of decisions that are behind the POLST (Physician Orders for Life-Sustaining Treatment) movement that has authorized a version of the POLST form in seventeen states).[50] But the POLST is not a complete care plan; it just provides physician orders to guide an emergency situation.

Frail elderly people and their families and surrogate decision-makers do not routinely articulate their goals and values, and when they do, substantial interpretation is usually required in order to translate them into a plan for services and actions. Asking baldly for what is most important to you at this stage of your life sometimes gets useful input, but sometimes gets tangential responses like, "Win the lottery." Usually, getting to understand a person's priorities takes some give and take in conversation. This requires substantial trust on the part of the frail elderly person and his or her family, and genuine empathy and engagement from at least the key service provider(s) on the care team.

People living with frailty and facing eventual death usually do not have just one goal—they have goals about relationships, spirituality, symptoms, finances, survival, and so on. We are complicated beings, after all. But the care team does need to come to understand the elderly person's perspective and the contribution of his or her family, and usually needs to condense the discussion into a small set of key goals for which actions of the care team (including the elderly person and family) can make a difference. These may be prosaic, as in, "I want to be able to walk to the mailbox," or they may be inspiring, as in, "I want to complete my last great painting." Characteristics of a helpful set of goal statements are these:

---

[50] (POLST 2015)

- That they actually reflect what matters most to the elderly person (and family),
- Achieving them is possible and is affected by the services provided, and
- One could know if they were achieved.

In addition to settling on the goals and priorities, the discussions that lead to good care plans have to settle on the services to be provided. Service selection is an endeavor that requires knowing what can be done for this elderly person and family at this time, how different plans are likely to affect the person, what sorts of services are acceptable to the elderly person and family, and what decisions they can be ready to make. Usually, the discussions of goals and services are iterative. Insights about what would be entailed to achieve a goal can affect the desirability of that goal. Insights about the desirability of particular goals can affect what service arrays are explored. Usually, the discussions end up with a convergence as to how to move ahead. Any shared decisions should be documented in a way that allows the responsible parties (including the elderly person and family) to re-visit the plan at particular future times or when needed. The documentation should articulate the goals and the agreed-upon strategies, as well as the key factors that contributed to the decisions.

The actual work of negotiating a care plan can take many forms. Sometimes, one skilled care team member and the elder or surrogate are the only ones involved. Sometimes, the negotiation can be done asynchronously by email and other communication devices. Often, the key team members all meet in person or by telecommunication to go over the situation together, to explore options, and to settle on a plan.[51]

Of course, in human interactions, not all situations come together well. Perhaps the family and elder do not trust the medical team, or the personal styles of interaction do not mesh well, or any of dozens of

---

[51] (Bokhour 2006)

other dysfunctions arise. In many cases, high-functioning care teams can creatively solve these problems, at least often enough that the vast majority of frail elderly people can have a workable care plan that is feasible, trustworthy, and allegiant to what matters most to the elder and family. PACE and hospice programs enjoy a good reputation for care plans that reflect the patients' values and priorities and guide care.

2.1.3 Setting parameters for re-evaluation

The care plan ordinarily includes planned re-evaluation and possible revision, usually at a specific time with a caveat for earlier review if anything unexpected arises or if the course is not working out as expected. The completeness and predictability of the care plan profoundly affect the anticipated timing for review. In a situation where much is not known about the elderly person's medical issues or when the elderly person does not wish to share information about living situation and desires, the care plan timetable may call for review much earlier than in a more favorable situation.

Care plans also can be rather fluid, as when a newly dependent elder is trying out a series of strategies to provide personal care, or when a challenging medical issue requires ongoing adjustment of treatment to pursue an optimal response. These modifications of details of the care plan need to be documented when they might affect other services and plans. Testing various strategies to learn which works best can also be made part of the care plan.

2.1.4 Assuring availability of the care plan across settings, providers, and time

The discussion above has made clear that the care plan, once agreed upon, should guide all services toward achieving the elderly person's priority goals. To accomplish that, the care plan itself needs to be available to key team members, including the elderly person and caregivers. This has proven to be quite difficult as frail elders move around from home to hospital and nursing home, or change home care attendants or physicians. One workable solution has been to give the elderly person or family caregiver a copy of the care plan to keep and take along. In just a few situations, such as PACE and hospice, all members of the care team are working in the same environment and can even stay involved when the elderly person is admitted to the hospital, so communication among the team is easy and is valued. But in the usual situation, the various parts of the service delivery system do not share records, do not even have compatible records, and often include both provider organizations that are covered by privacy laws and provider organizations that are not. These issues incur substantial problems that only will be solved by the eventual interoperability of records and inclusion of organizations providing services like housing, transportation, and personal care. In the meantime, creative interim solutions suitable for each setting will have to suffice.

Piloting of interoperable health care records for frail elders in the community is underway. The Office of the National Coordinator for Health Information Technology has coordinated a confederation of volunteer groups working on these problems. The scope of the care plans they are working with is still very short-term and tied to transitions in setting of care, but they have standardized the elements of a record format likely to support more comprehensive and longitudinal care plans. For example, Maryland's health information exchange (CRISP, at *crisphealth.org*) is developing a way to incorporate a care profile into the notification process for a person who uses a hospital. This standardized care profile includes recent utilization, medications and other treatments, diagnoses, demographic data, advance directives, and contact information. In addition, if a documented care plan exists, it can be available through a link in the care profile.

The nation's hospitals and physician offices have been able to obtain substantial financial support for adopting electronic records, so long as they meet certain standards.[52] Unfortunately for frail elders, providers of long-term services and supports are not included in this

---

[52] (Office of the National Coordinator for Health Information Technology, Meaningful Use Stage 3, 80 FR 62648 2015)

program, and the requirements thus far only include information adequate to facilitate safe transfers from one setting to another. Communities that aim to adopt a MediCaring model will need to assess their community's capacity for interoperable records and devise a strategy that enables reasonable continuity and comprehensiveness as well as 24/7/365 access.

2.1.5 Dealing with difficulties in care planning

Care planning can go awry in a variety of ways. Elders and their families can refuse to be engaged; critical information about likely future course can be ignored or simply unavailable; the care team can be too hard to convene; the discussion can end up with no decisions; the care plan developed can become unavailable when needed; and so on. The communities implementing MediCaring Communities need to understand that developing efficient and effective methods to generate care plans at scale for frail elders will be a work-in-progress, with much to learn in the next few years.

One pervasive problem is that the understanding of the elderly person's situation and choices could always be more detailed, no matter how much is already known; but overload of information makes the information as useless as a deficit of information. Sending a frail elderly person to the emergency room with one hundred pages of copied records will induce the emergency room staff to set the whole stack aside, given the press of time and the need to prioritize urgent matters. The "presentation layer" for care planning needs much more attention from creative minds, aiming to show the most salient things, as well as a general overview, depending upon the focus of the user. The elderly person viewing his or her own care plan generally does not care to read the history and may be overwhelmed with medical or administrative details, but he or she very well may want an explanation of the goals of medications and a characterization of the likely course. The emergency room physician usually does not need to know the details of nutrition support at home. A set of streamlined presentations would make the care plan and its background information so much more useful, though the user also needs to be able to pursue important issues more deeply when warranted.

Good care planning also needs much more useful information about prognosis, both for survival and for function. Predictions of outcome often depend mostly on the physician's experience, and physicians rarely follow elderly patients over time, so they really don't know what the likely course will be and what supportive services the person will need. An intriguing website at *http://eprognosis.ucsf.edu/* gives some approximations of likely survival time. The website does not give a sense of the "shape of the curve," just the point estimate for when half of the people "like this person" will have died, and it does not address function and therefore supportive service needs.[53] With all the data that Medicare now has access to, and the enhanced data arriving with the IMPACT Act, Medicare could generate a set of interactive data analyses that would allow estimates of likely outcomes, given various treatment strategies.[54] Having accurate data on the likelihood of future disabilities and death will be disheartening to some, but it would be very helpful to all involved, since honest and reliable information is essential to preventing emergencies and being prepared for the likely future course.

The measure of success in the care plan cannot be simply whether the elderly person achieved his or her priority goals. Some elderly persons and families will insist upon pursuing very unlikely goals—to live for another five years or to be able to live alone, perhaps. We need to establish a process that does not force elders and families to accept easy goals or encourage them to state outlandish ones. What may become the standard for good care is whether the care team helps them pursue the goals as promised and whether the elderly person and family were confident that what mattered most to them was the highest priority of the care team as well. Developing efficient ways to measure elder-driven dimensions of quality will be an important component of MediCaring implementation.

---

[53] (Lee, et al. n.d.)
[54] (Improving Medicare Post-Acute Transformation Act of 2014, Public Law 113-185 2014)

Finally, some assessment instruments automatically trigger care plan elements. The most well known of these is probably the MDS (for nursing home residents) for which certain responses about the elderly person's situation trigger elements of the expected care plan.[55] This approach may be useful for certain widely acceptable strategies, such as providing pressure-reducing mattresses for persons at high risk of pressure ulcers. However, most treatment strategies require input from the elderly person or their representative, so the automatic nature of the triggering leads to work-arounds and inaccuracies in the record. For example, documenting that the resident has a depressive mood disorder triggers a deficiency in MDS if the person is not on a medication to address depression. But many nursing home residents have tried anti-depressants and don't want to do so again, so the nurse entering the data is induced to circumvent the appearance of a deficiency by noting that the resident is sad, but not acknowledging depression. This sort of adverse incentive reduces the value of the record and the care plan and must be avoided if possible in developing work processes and tools for care planning.

2.2 How could the delivery system evaluate and improve the care planning process?

A hallmark of a high-functioning system is that monitoring the quality of the processes and the products is a built-in part of the workflow, as is taking steps to improve and to address shortcomings. In well-engineered production systems, feedback loops to upstream contributors are commonplace and valued. This kind of integration of the system and enabling of management appears to be completely missing with regard to care planning for frail elder care. A responsible manager would want to monitor such elements as the presence of a documented care plan, its effective implementation, the accuracy of the

---

[55] (Centers for Medicare and Medicaid Services, MDS 3.0 RAI Manual 2016)

information on which it was based, the articulation and achievement of the priority goals, and the confidence felt by the elderly person and family. Not only should such elements be monitored, but those responsible for building a care plan need to learn how the situation turned out and to be enabled to improve performance because they have feedback from which to learn.

Metrics of this sort are profoundly underdeveloped. A few teams monitor existence of a care plan, requiring a few key elements. Some individuals and teams follow up to see how things turned out. But Medicare's list of 992 metrics now in use does not include even a single element on care plans except for the limited settings with limited statutory requirements.[56] Indeed, no Medicare measures of quality incorporate the elderly person's own preferences and goals in the evaluation of performance.

So, concerned persons should push for better metrics; involved caregivers and providers should engender processes that provide feedback; and elderly persons should have the care plans that reflect their situation and preferences.

2.3 How could the delivery system use care plans to improve the service supply and quality?

Once a community has care planning working for most frail elderly people in a population and has a way to aggregate defined elements electronically, then the community has the makings of a remarkable tool for managing the service supply and quality for that population. With multiple communities, the method would allow benchmarking supply against demand (since oversupply is often as problematic as undersupply), geo-mapping service demand and availability and testing for mis-matches, detecting perceptions of quality or delay problems, and more. If the care planning process

---

[56] (Centers for Medicare and Medicaid Services Measures Inventory 2016)

includes making note of the compromises that inadequate supply or quality has required, then the aggregation can also tally those shortcomings as real-time evidence of problems. What follows is our first working out of a method to manage the service supply arrangements for a community, fueled by care plans.

This example is meant just to show the possibilities for community-based management. Having most frail elders' care plans would allow development of a powerful method for monitoring and managing the supply and quality of services for the whole community's frail elderly population. If the care plans also recorded the compromises caused by shortages or quality problems, that will create a method for weighing priorities among possible improvement activities.

In short, care planning is essential, though sometimes difficult, and many forces are converging to push care providers serving elderly persons living with chronic conditions to build elder-driven care plans.

Figure 2.2: Optimizing a Service Production System

How many frail elderly? Estimates here for a hypothetical community of 600,000 residents are roughly supported by research and experience. A useful model for a specific community would need the actual targeted population, including population metrics of the rates of frailty and disability and the expected case load for the workforce. The point here is to illustrate the powerful tool that a community could develop from aggregating the care plans of their frail elders.

- In a community of 600,000 residents, about 6,000 die each year, about 5,000 in old age.
  - About 2,500 die of a single overwhelming disease (generally appropriate for hospice and needing little long-term care or complicated planning for supportive services).
  - About 2,500 die of frailty, including multiple chronic conditions and advanced illness complicated by supportive service needs.
- Substantial self-care disability for frail elders will last an average of two years before death.
- Thus, at any one time, about 5,000 frail adults >65 years of age will be in need of supportive services in the last years of life.

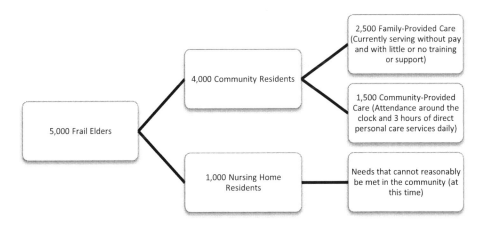

Table 2.1: Workforce Example: Estimating Primary Care Providers Doing Home Visits

Number of home visits

- 4,000 people living with serious frailty in the community
- Routine visit every 4 months
- Urgent visit 3/year
- 4,000 X 6 = 24,000 home visits needed

Primary Care Provider (PCP) Requirements

- Can see ~10 visits/day (with assistant/driver)
- ~240 days per year
- 10 X 240 = 2,400 visits / PCP /year
- The community needs 10 full-time PCPs (and 10 full-time assistants/drivers) to serve frail elders at home.
- They can also provide 24/7 coverage for urgent situations by cross-covering out-of-hours calls.

Table 2.2: Estimates for others in the workforce for the sample community

	1,000 Nursing Home Elders	4,000 Community Elders
Direct Care Workers	500 (at a 1:6 ratio, 3 shifts, all year)	800 (at about 3 hours/elder/weekday, plus travel and time off)
Nurses	100	500
Therapists	100	100
Primary Care Providers (PCPs)	5	10
Drivers and Scribes	0	10
Hospital Beds	50	250

Core Component #3: Medical Care Tailored to Frail Elders

All too often, the medical care that frail elders get is indefensibly poorly considered. Nursing home residents near death, who have no real odds of getting a net benefit from hospitalization, are moved to hospitals as "emergencies" to evaluate fevers or not eating.[57] Slightly healthier frail elders are regularly given medications that are contraindicated in the elderly, or sent for screening tests that cannot yield benefit in the remaining lifespan.[58,59] Anxious or cognitively impaired elders who are mostly scared or overwhelmed are treated with sedating and mind-altering medications.[60] Elders living with fragile arrangements for caregiving have those disrupted by physician insistence on seeing patients in the office (or hospital). Physicians might insist upon seeing only the frail elder, leaving the family caregiver in the waiting room with critical information; or they might see the frail elder but talk only to the family caregiver, thus offending and perhaps silencing the patient and that person's store of relevant information. Many busy clinicians simply won't deal with the array of issues that a frail elderly person presents and will insist upon dealing with only a couple at any one visit, thus precluding a real care plan. Indeed, very few physicians want to or know how to generate a good care plan for frail elders.

Sometimes, the current focus on healthy communities and social determinants of health seems to marginalize the experience of frailty, decline and death. The claims for the merits of various improvements in population exercise, diet, housing, jobs, and so forth would seem to eliminate the experience of serious illness. However, mortality is an

---

[57] (J. Ouslander, et al. 2010)

[58] (Caverly, et al. 2015)

[59] (Lee, et al. 2013)

[60] (United States Government Accountability Office, Antipsychotic Drug Use: HHS Has Initiatives to Reduce Use among Older Adults in Nursing Homes, but Should Expand Efforts to Other Settings 2015)

unyielding part of the human experience. Preventing various illnesses earlier in life is actually giving rise to the increasing number of people living with frailty and decline. Living well in the shadow of death, and living well with disabilities and decline, are certainly possible and actually provide the focus of MediCaring approaches. Much of the care plan addresses preventing complications, exacerbations, crises, suffering, and travail. Physicians, as well as elderly individuals and their communities, will learn much in the coming years as to what counts as living well in the last years of life, limited by disabilities and chronic conditions.

This chapter responds to these key questions:

3.1 What are the critical elements of geriatricized medical services?

3.2 How would MediCaring Communities develop the workforce?

3.3 How could MediCaring Communities encourage elders to use clinicians who provide geriatricized medical care?

3.4 What is already known about how to improve medical services for frail elders?

3.1 What are the critical elements of geriatricized medical services?

A good geriatricized medical service should have all of the following components.

☑ Always committed to an elder-driven care plan, appropriately comprehensive

As developed above, the point of good geriatric care is not generally to align with professional standards that were established with "average" patients, but to develop and implement the customized plan that helps frail elderly people to live as well as possible, from their own perspectives, despite various disabilities and constraints. For frail elders, a good care plan always includes guidance as to treatments and concerns around the time of death—an advance care plan, for end-of-life care.

☑ Alignment with the elderly person's goals, and the family's

Good care requires knowing what matters most to the elderly person and family, and arranging services so that they are confident that their care team is "on my side," and seeking what is best, as defined by the elderly person and family. For example, this requires awareness of how much the frail elder often loses in strength or cognitive function just by going into the hospital. Furthermore, the elder may lose a well-functioning set of supportive services and home care aides. Thus, deciding to go to the hospital becomes a weighty decision guided by the options for and risks of treatment at home, judged from the perspective of the elder's priorities.

☑ Providers skilled at working in a team and negotiating care plans, whether as leader or member

Multidisciplinary teams whose focus is frail elders will coordinate elder-driven care in the MediCaring Community. Such teams are already required in PACE and hospice, and are often found in nursing homes also. Effective teams include clinicians and practitioners trained and skilled in a broad array of activities: diagnosis and treatment; medication management; rehabilitation; self-care; nursing care; mental health; caregiver assessment, training, and support; nutrition; community services; and housing. Teams would generally include a physician, nurse, and social worker as core participants with the elderly person and family, and they can rely upon ongoing and reliable access to pharmacists, rehabilitation specialists, mental health experts, housing services staff, caregiver support personnel, and legal advisors. The team's capabilities and functioning would be measured and certified as meeting standards that reflect well-coordinated care, rather than mainly monitoring adherence to requirements for certain disciplines doing certain tasks. Over time, high functioning teams acquire a great deal of cross-training, so disciplinary boundaries become blurred.

☑ Honest and accurate about prognosis and options

Currently, practitioners do not often have the information needed to characterize the likely futures for the elderly person, and, even when they do, they do not generally share that information with the elderly person and family. Some of this is a polite effort to maintain optimism and hopefulness, and some reflects the general lack of familiarity with making decisions while informed of the likelihood of various outcomes. The lack of accurate information could be addressed with analyses of large data sets as to the course of relevantly similar people who were in the same situation a few years ago. But we still need to generate a shared sense that elderly people and their families deserve the opportunity to make their own decisions as adults, and therefore to have honest information, even if the situation presents a grim or upsetting picture.

☑ Deep empathy with the challenges of loss, cognitive failure, compromises, and death

Providing care for frail elderly people always ends in the person's death and usually entails a long course of decline. To care for persons who cannot "get better" and who will die requires substantial maturity and dedication, but providing services and support is essential. The loneliness of old age is, perhaps, even more devastating than the loss of muscle strength or the diminishment of hearing. A good community would make it possible for caregivers, neighbors, and friends to know and truly care about the elderly person, not just to accomplish the tasks necessary to mere survival.

☑ On-call 24/7 with a person known to elder and family and with care plan in hand

MediCaring requires continuity of services across time, settings, and providers, with round-the-clock coverage and real-time availability to the elder and his or her caregivers. A MediCaring team would be charged with providing medical and nursing advice and support. In the case of an urgent phone call (or text or email) with a pressing health concern, a team member with appropriate skills for the problem would respond promptly. The team member on call would often know the elder and caregivers personally and would always have immediate access to an up-to-date care plan.

☑ Able to provide routine and urgent services in the elder's home (including nursing home)

Frail elders and their caregivers can be stressed and overwhelmed by the challenge of simply getting to a physician's office. Whenever feasible, urgent home visits to assess emerging situations should occur within three hours of a call (or, in rural or otherwise difficult areas, telemedicine should be planned and used). The process of developing care plans for MediCaring elders should include honest and forthright understanding about when and if to call 911 or to go to an emergency department. For frail, homebound elders, many technical and supportive services, guided by a competent physical examination, can be safely done where the elderly person lives, including simple diagnostic x-rays and other imaging, blood and urine tests, skin biopsies, electrocardiograms, and more. This spares frail elders the burdens and risks of being moved to another setting simply to receive good medical care, especially when that care can so effectively be delivered to them where they live. Home visits are a wise, safe, and effective method for preventing or delaying hospitalizations and nursing home placements. For example, preliminary results from the Independence at Home demonstration, which delivers primary care at home, show clear benefits to elders, who have fewer hospitalizations and ED visits, as well as fewer 30-day readmissions.[61] In the interests of prudent spending, any service that works in multiple elderly person's homes has to consider the possibility of organizing delivery of services geographically, rather than having a large array of providers of the same service competing. The practice of having a large number of competing services is usually justified by a claim that this will hold down prices and improve quality (or at least customer service). In health care for frail elders at home, this claim is a weak one since so much of the productive time of skilled people ends up being spent in transportation, and the clients have so little interest in or accessible information about quality that competition has little effect.

☑ Avoidance of preventable complications—falls, dehydration, medication errors, unwanted CPR

Much of good geriatric care focuses upon prevention – not often prevention of the underlying physical problem, but prevention of the complications. Elders have very little resilience to withstand errors, so medications must be carefully considered and adjusted, for example. Falls are a scourge, both because of injuries and because falling makes the person hesitant to walk around, which reduces capacity for ambulation over time. Many falls are preventable, both by monitoring medications and blood pressure and by arranging the home environment to be protective, e.g., with good lighting, no trip hazards,

---

[61] (Centers for Medicare and Medicaid Services, Independence at Home (IAH) Demonstration: Year 1 Practice Results 2015)

and hand rails.[62] Of course, one also and obviously wants to avoid aggressive medical interventions like resuscitation, dialysis, and ventilators unless they really offer the person an advantage and the well-informed elderly person wants them used.

☑ Broad knowledge of specialty medicine to be able to integrate specialty perspectives

The geriatric physician or nurse practitioner truly must be a "comprehensivist"—a clinician able to understand and manage the contributions of specialist physicians and therapists and being responsible for forging that all-important care plan with the elderly person and family. Not all clinicians care to take on this role. It requires being able to ask for help often, as well as have well-honed sensibilities as to what works, in what situations, and with what outcomes.

☑ Attention to important disabilities not covered by Medicare

One can readily discern that the scope of Medicare coverage was not established by frail elders—it does not attend to hearing, vision, teeth, or feet. A geriatric approach to medical care has to address these issues, since they cause so much suffering and isolation to elders. The geriatric medical provider needs to be able to screen for problems in these arenas and the team has to know how to obtain services from practitioners who are sensitive to the needs and priorities of frail elders, including dealing with issues about costs and personal finances.

---

[62] (Tinetti and Kumar 2010)

☑ **Aware of and engaged with the supportive services in the community**

A geriatric clinician will quickly become aware of the strengths and gaps in the community's supportive services (LTSS). This will help steer care plans toward effective and available services, but it also will call on the geriatrician and the team to be engaged with advocating for optimizing the supply and quality of services in their community. MediCaring teams will monitor quality and supply and will be present at governmental hearings and philanthropic decision-making in order to move their community toward adequate supply and reliable quality.

3.2 How would MediCaring Communities develop the workforce?

In just about every area, some physicians are already providing good care to frail elderly people, despite adverse incentives and challenges. MediCaring Communities would identify those clinicians and teams and build on their successes. Other primary care physicians might well want to follow their lead and focus effectively on the special needs of these very fragile patients. Often, the challenges of serving this population are made even worse when the quality measures in use are misleading. Medicare's quality metrics at this point are inattentive to personal preferences, calibrated for preventing illnesses and complications in persons with conventionally long lives, and focused entirely on health outcomes. Obviously, the metrics needed for frail elders would start with personal preferences, would adjust to the limited expectation of survival time, and would balance joys and satisfactions in living with realistically limited possibilities for health outcomes. It should be high-quality care to allow a frail elder to eat what is satisfying, to ignore long-term complications of hypertension and diabetes, and to avoid troublesome cancer screening and prevention strategies that have little chance of affecting their remaining lives. But this approach will lead to the physician being judged wrongly to be providing poor quality care.

So, the MediCaring Community could act to remove or reduce some of these barriers and thereby enable a broader set of primary care physicians to serve frail elders well.[63] Most areas will need a service to provide medical care at home. The home-based primary care model from the Veterans Health Administration is very appealing.[64] Implementing the model more broadly in Independence at Home has gone well.[65,66] Generally, patients will need to shift into this model as it becomes too difficult to come to the doctor's office. In order to be available to the homebound population and to capitalize on efficiencies of not supporting the overhead of a conventional office, the home-based primary care physician may do best to focus upon this delivery mode, rather than doing home visits during or after office hours.

The Hartford Institute for Geriatric Nursing has developed or referenced a remarkable array of resources, which make it easier to excel at training nurses to serve frail elders with confidence and high standards.[67]

The workforce issues are especially serious for personal care, particularly of persons with dementia. Personal care aides usually have very little training and mostly work without direct supervision. They often come from very different backgrounds than their elderly clients and their families, so language and culture may clash. And the jobs are dramatically underpaid, so many aides work two jobs or very long hours, just to pay essential bills. MediCaring Communities might well undertake to provide more training, a more reasonable wage and benefit structure, and a career ladder, if the availability of skilled aides is a priority concern.

---

[63] (American Geriatrics Society Expert Panel on the Care of Older Adults 2012)

[64] (Edes, et al. 2014)

[65] (Centers for Medicare and Medicaid Services, Independence at Home (IAH) Demonstration: Year 1 Practice Results 2015)

[66] (Centers for Medicare and Medicaid Services, Affordable Care Act payment model saves more than $25 million in first performance year 2015)

[67] (Hartford Institute for Geriatric Nursing 2016)

Of course, all of the people providing services need to know the special characteristics of elders in general and of the particular elderly person they are serving. From wound healing to dementia behaviors to dentures and hearing aids, being old and frail is different and requires adjustment of the usual approaches.

3.3 How could MediCaring Communities encourage elders to use clinicians who provide geriatricized medical care?

MediCaring builds on and ensures primary care for elders who live with advanced, serious, and complex conditions. Primary care for frail elders is not primary care as usual, which is often a doctor who provides routine prevention services, a limited amount of chronic disease self-care education, treatment for minor illnesses and injuries, and coordination of services from specialists. In contrast, geriatric clinical practice is primary care for some of the most complicated patient situations, responsive and responsible in recognizing and assuring that the service array meets the important and interacting physical, psychosocial, and spiritual needs that very complicated elders and their families encounter.[68] But elderly persons and their families do not know this. They believe that any physician is as capable as another, and that there is no reason to consider leaving the physician who served them through mid-life just because they are becoming old and frail. That physician is unlikely to have many of the check-mark characteristics discussed earlier in this chapter, probably has no particular training in geriatric or end-of-life care, and probably is used to having short visits with patients (often 10-15 minutes), which does not allow time for dealing with complex issues.

The MediCaring Community could institute incentives to encourage use of the more skilled and appropriate medical providers. This could take the form of a list of preferred providers, a financial

---

[68] (Tinetti, Fried and Boyd 2012)

incentive for using them, information as to the merits of various providers, publicity in local media, and word-of-mouth recommendations. The community could also provide feedback to the practitioners as to the quality of their services and could offer ongoing education and tools to encourage appropriate geriatric standards.

The first MediCaring Communities may be developed by expanding certain PACE programs, which is a very appealing first implementation that is described in detail in Chapter 7. In that setting, the PACE program would take on some responsibility to monitor and manage the workforce and other needs in the community.

3.4 What is already known about how to improve medical services for frail elders?

A number of elder care reform programs have demonstrated improvements in care for frail elders by, for example, providing comprehensive care planning, provision of services in the home when appropriate, and ensuring access to community-based services. These programs have reduced use of hospitals and nursing homes and improved quality of life for frail elderly people. The summary below provides evidence for the effectiveness of some of the most prominent programs. As you will see in these examples, there is no shortage of proven strategies. What is missing is the means for financing and spread, which the MediCaring Communities approach provides and which we will explain in Chapters 6 and 7.

Table 3.1: Evidence-Based Clinical Improvement Examples

Here is a summary of findings on some of the prominent and proven improvements in geriatric medical care that are relevant to the MediCaring Communities model. A MediCaring Community can implement any of these strategies and eventually will incorporate the core improvements in these and more. For each intervention we summarize a description, the evidence for effectiveness, and the evidence for cost savings (when available).

Program of All-Inclusive Care for the Elderly (PACE)

Description: Provides health care and LTSS to nursing home eligible seniors 55 and up. Interdisciplinary care teams provide care management and plan service delivery based on each enrollee's assessed needs. Nearly all enrollees have dual capitation: both Medicare and Medicaid. The PACE program is responsible for all necessary services. The PACE program has been Congressionally authorized for about 30 years and has grown to serving about 35,000 elders.[69] PACE enjoys a good reputation for quality, reliability, and comprehensiveness but has been very slow to replicate. In some states the program is called Living Independence for the Elderly (LIFE). The possibilities of building the MediCaring Community on the PACE foundation are explained in Chapter 7. Read more at *http://www.npaonline.org*.

Evidence for Effectiveness:

- Enrollees compared to similarly frail community-dwelling older adults over a 2-year period showed PACE enrollees had 75% less hospital utilization per enrollee.[70]

- PACE enrollees were also less likely to experience pain that interferes with their routine ($p<.01$) and had better self-reported health than a comparison group in a Home and Community-Based Service (HCBS) program ($p<.01$).[71]

- PACE enrollees were also significantly less likely than the comparison group to have unmet needs in getting around (8%, $p<.05$), bathing (8%, $p<.01$), and dressing (6%, $p<.05$).

---

[69] (National PACE Association n.d.)
[70] (Meret-Hanke 2011)
[71] (Beauchamp, et al. 2008)

Cost-Savings Evidence:

- PACE's Medicaid capitation was 28% lower than predicted fee for service payments for similar patients in alternative LTSS programs.[72]
- Another study found a 14% reduction in the months using nursing homes.[73] Since social service needs have no clear boundary, PACE is not expected to save overall costs beyond establishing a reasonable operating reserve. Instead, PACE is expected to serve beneficiaries much better than the usual poorly coordinated and planned service array and to stay within current costs.

Aetna Compassionate Care Program

Description: Care managers (CM) completed a comprehensive assessment of the patient's needs, provided education and support, gave assistance with pain medications and psychosocial needs, and helped ensure that advance directives were in place and implemented. Some beneficiaries were given expanded hospice benefits, including receipt of "curative treatment" (aggressive or disease-targeted treatment that is usually not part of hospice care).[74]

Evidence for Effectiveness:

- Hospice use increased 30.8% to 71.7% for all groups receiving CM compared to control groups, and from 27.9% to 69.8% for the group with CM and enhanced hospice benefits.
- All groups receiving CM had between 40 and 85% fewer acute hospital days per thousand members compared

---

[72] (Wieland, et al. 2013)

[73] (JEN Associates 2013)

[74] You can read more about the Aetna Compassionate Care Program at: *https://www.aetna.com/individuals-families/member-rights-resources/compassionate-care-program.html.*

with their historical control groups ($p<.0001$ for all). Medicare Advantage members receiving CM had 2,309 hospital days per thousand members versus 15,217 per thousand members for those not receiving CM ($p<.0001$).[75]

Cost-Savings Evidence:

- Estimated net cost decrease of 22% for Aetna's commercially insured population compared with a historical control group.[76]

The Bridge Model

Description: Social work-based transitional care intervention that begins in the hospital and continues after discharge to the community. It includes biopsychosocial assessment, integration of psychotherapeutic techniques into care coordination and case management activities to increase patient engagement in their own care, and a standardized approach to hospital-community-Aging Network collaboration.

Evidence for Effectiveness:

- 20% reduction in 30 day readmissions compared with controls who did not receive Bridge services ($p<.05$).[77]

Care Transitions Intervention®

Description: During a 4-week program, patients with complex care needs receive specific tools, are supported by a Transitions Coach®, and learn self-management skills to ensure their needs are met during the transition from hospital to home.[78]

---

[75] (Spettell, et al. 2009)
[76] (Krakauer, et al. 2009)
[77] (Boutwell, Johnson and Watkins in press)
[78] You can read more about the Care Transitions Intervention® at *http://caretransitions.org.*

Evidence for Effectiveness:

- Patients in one trial had reduced rehospitalization rates at 30 days(8.3% vs 11.9%, *p*=.048) and 90 days (16.7% vs 22.5% *p*=.04).[79]

Cost-Savings Evidence:

- Mean hospital costs were lower for patients in the CTI program ($2,058 vs $2,546, *p*=.049).[80]

Geriatric Resources for Assessment and Care of Elders (GRACE)

Description: Advanced practice nurse and social worker care for low-income seniors in collaboration with the patient's primary care physician and a geriatrics interdisciplinary team. The program includes comprehensive geriatric assessment by the GRACE support team, an individualized care plan, and a home visit by the nurse and social worker. GRACE uses a set of evidence-based protocols to manage a number of specified geriatric conditions.[81]

Evidence for Effectiveness:

- Decreased emergency department (ED) utilization rates by 5% (year 1), 35% (year 2), and 21% (year 3, post-intervention) for those at highest risk of hospitalization.[82]

Cost-Savings Evidence:

- Randomized controlled trial of GRACE in primary care health centers enrolling 951 low-income seniors aged 65+. Increased primary care costs but reduced hospital costs; Group that showed high risk of hospitalization

---

[79] (Coleman, et al. 2006)

[80] (Coleman, et al. 2006)

[81] You can read more about Geriatric Resources for Assessment and Care of Elders (GRACE) at *http://graceteamcare.indiana.edu/home.html*.

[82] (Hong, Siegel and Ferris 2014)

averaged net savings of $1,487 per person-year or 23% in the third year ($5,088 vs. $6,575; $p<.001$).[83]

Guided Care®

Description: Registered nurse works with two to five physicians in a primary care practice to provide high-risk multi-morbid patients with eight services: home-based assessment of patients' needs and goals, evidence-based care planning, proactive monitoring, care coordination, transitional care, coaching for self-management, caregiver support, and access to community-based services.[84]

Evidence for Effectiveness:

- 6% reduction in hospital admissions;
- 13% reduction in 30-day hospital re-admissions;
- 26% fewer skilled nursing facility days.[85]

Cost-Savings Evidence:

- One cluster-randomized controlled trial found that Guided Care produced a net savings of $75,000 per Guided Care Nurse per year.[86]

Hospital at Home Program

Description: Patients requiring hospital-level treatment receive appropriate diagnostic exams and treatments in the home.[87]

Evidence for Effectiveness:

- Patients and family members in the Hospital at Home group rated their satisfaction on a number of care domains

---

[83] (Counsell, et al. 2009)

[84] You can read more about Guided Care® at *http://www.guidedcare.org.*

[85] (Boult, et al. 2013)

[86] (Leff, Reider, et al. 2009)

[87] You can read more about the Hospital at Home Program at *http://www.hospitalathome.org.*

significantly more highly than those in the control group. Ratings were higher for Hospital at Home patients on a median of 7 domains compared with 6 domains for the control group ($p<.001$) and a median of 6 vs. 5 domains ($p<.001$) for family members.

Cost-Savings Evidence:

- The mean cost of care was significantly lower for hospital-at-home care than for acute hospital care ($5,081 vs. $7,480) ($p<.001$).[88]

Independence at Home

Description: Primary care practices provide home-based primary care to chronically ill beneficiaries with ADL limitations and prior hospitalizations for a three-year period, and make in-home visits tailored to an individual patient's needs and coordinate their care. This is a congressionally authorized demonstration program.[89]

Evidence for Effectiveness:

- Beneficiaries have fewer hospital readmissions within 30 days;
- Participants are more likely to have their preferences documented by their provider; and to use inpatient hospital and emergency department services less.[90]

Cost-Savings Evidence:

- Demonstration showed overall cost savings of $25 million, and an average of $3,070 per beneficiary in its first year.[91]

---

[88] (Leff, Burton, et al. 2005)

[89] You can read more about Independence at Home at *https://innovation.cms.gov/-initiatives/independence-at-home*.

[90] (Centers for Medicare and Medicaid Services, Affordable Care Act payment model saves more than $25 million in first performance year 2015)

Interventions to Reduce Acute Care Transfers (INTERACT)

Description: This program provides a set of evidence-based clinical practice tools and strategies to reduce hospitalizations from nursing homes (NH). The model includes identifying, assessing, and managing conditions proactively to prevent them from becoming severe, managing selected conditions in the NH, and improving advance care planning.[92]

Evidence for Effectiveness:

- 25 NHs that completed the 6-month INTERACT II intervention had a 17% reduction in hospitalization rates ($p=.02$).[93]

Cost-Savings Evidence:

- Estimated Medicare savings of intervention in a 100-bed nursing home would be about $125,000 per year.[94]

Project RED (Re-Engineered Discharge)

Description: A nurse discharge advocate works with patients during their hospital stay to arrange follow-up appointments, confirm medications reconciliation, and conduct patient education with an individualized instruction booklet. A clinical pharmacist calls patients 2 to 4 days after discharge to review medications.

Evidence for Effectiveness:

- Participants receiving the RED intervention had a 30% lower rate of hospital utilization than those receiving usual care. ($p<.01$)[95]

---

[91] (Centers for Medicare and Medicaid Services, Affordable Care Act payment model saves more than $25 million in first performance year 2015)

[92] You can read more about Interventions to Reduce Acute Care Transfers (INTERACT) at *http://interact2.net/*.

[93] (J. G. Ouslander, et al. 2011)

[94] (J. G. Ouslander, et al. 2011)

Cost-Savings Evidence:
- Costs were 33.9% lower for those receiving the intervention, an average savings of $412 per person.[96]

Sutter Health Advanced Illness Management (AIM) Program

Description: AIM is an integrated system of care for patients with late-stage chronic illnesses that provides home-based transitional and palliative care and counsels patients and families with the goal of increasing hospice use and decreasing the use of unwanted acute care.[97]

Evidence for Effectiveness:
- Hospice referral was compared between AIM enrollees and two Usual Care cohorts, one drawn from the same home health branch as the AIM program (Usual Care I), and one drawn from a demographically similar Sutter branch without AIM (Usual Care II). 28% more AIM enrollees were referred to hospice compared with Usual Care I, ($p<.003$) and 67% more than Usual Care II ($p<.0001$).[98]
- 413 AIM patients who lived at least 90 days following enrollment experienced 54 % fewer hospitalizations over those 90 days compared with the 90-day period before enrollment. Over the same period, intensive care unit days were reduced by 80 percent and length of stay on subsequent admissions was reduced by 26 percent.[99]

---

[95] (Jack, et al. 2009)
[96] (Jack, et al. 2009)
[97] You can read more about the Sutter Health Advanced Illness Management (AIM) Program at *http://www.sutterhealth.org/quality/focus/advanced-illness-management.html.*
[98] (Ciemens, et al. 2006)
[99] (Agency for Healthcare Research and Quality 2013)

Cost-Savings Evidence:

The program resulted in cost savings to Medicare of $760 per AIM enrollee per month, and Net health system savings amounted to $213 per enrollee per month.[100]

Veteran's Affairs Home-Based Primary Care (HBPC)

Description: Program serves aging Veterans with complex chronic diseases in their homes. Target population is simply "too sick to come to clinic." The services include primary care visits at home, care planning, coordination of services by a social worker, and caregiver support.[101]

Evidence for Effectiveness:

- HBPC veterans had 59% reduction in hospital bed days of care and 89% reduction in nursing home bed days of care.[102]

- VA and Medicare-paid hospitalizations combined were 25.5% lower than observed without home-based primary care.[103]

Cost-Savings Evidence:

- The HBPC program provided a mean total VA cost of care decrease of 24% in 2002 ($38,000 to $29,000 per patient per year). ($p<.001$).[104]

- During HBPC program Medicare costs were 10.8% lower than projected, and VA plus Medicare costs were 11.7% lower.[105]

---

[100] (Agency for Healthcare Research and Quality 2013)
[101] You can read more about Veteran's Affairs Home-Based Primary Care (HBPC) at *http://www.va.gov/geriatrics/guide/longtermcare/home_based_primary_care.asp.*
[102] (Beales and Edes 2009)
[103] (Edes, et al. 2014)
[104] (Beales and Edes 2009)
[105] (Edes, et al. 2014)

Core Component #4: Integrating Social and Supportive Services

For the last fifty years in the United States, medical care for elders has been enjoying very nearly a blank check from Medicare, with few effective constraints on utilization and a general cultural attitude that supports "leaving no stone unturned" by pursuing even long odds of benefit from medical services. On the other hand, supportive services for elders have been provided erratically, mostly as safety net programs, with little evaluation and many widely ignored gaps.

Bradley and Taylor showed that the U.S. spends about the same proportion of GDP on the combination of medical, social, and supportive services as most developed countries, but the U.S. uniquely spends much more on medical care (nearly double) and much less on social and supportive services (about half).[106] Figures 4.1 and 4.2 show the ratio of health spending to social service spending for several major countries.

---

[106] (Bradley and Taylor 2013, pp. 4-14) The OECD and the authors define health service expenditures as public and private spending on curative care, rehabilitative care, long-term care (not including personal care and ADL assistance), ancillary services such as diagnostic imaging, lab tests and patient transport, outpatient medical goods, prevention and public health services, health administration, and health insurance and healthcare capital expenditures. Social services expenditures include public and private spending on old-age pension and support services for older adults, survivors benefits, disability and sickness cash benefits, family supports, employment programs such as public employment services and employment training, unemployment benefits, supportive housing and rent subsidies, and other social services that exclude health expenditures.

Figure 4.1: Health Service and Social Service Spending (% of GDP)[107]

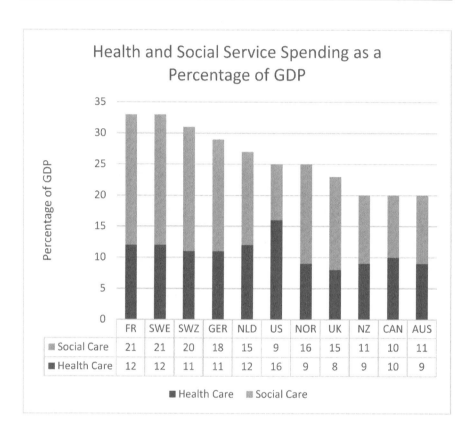

Health and Social Service Spending as a Percentage of GDP

	FR	SWE	SWZ	GER	NLD	US	NOR	UK	NZ	CAN	AUS
Social Care	21	21	20	18	15	9	16	15	11	10	11
Health Care	12	12	11	11	12	16	9	8	9	10	9

■ Health Care   ■ Social Care

---

[107] Figures 4.1 and 4.2 are based on data in Bradley and Taylor 2013, pp. 15 and 17. "GDP" refers to Gross Domestic Product.

Figure 4.2: Ratio of Social to Health Service Spending (% of GDP)

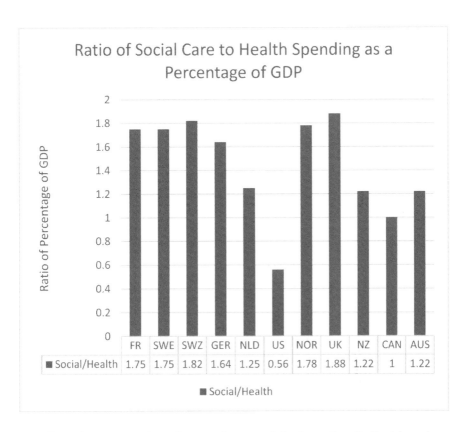

Ratio of Social Care to Health Spending as a Percentage of GDP

	FR	SWE	SWZ	GER	NLD	US	NOR	UK	NZ	CAN	AUS
■ Social/Health	1.75	1.75	1.82	1.64	1.25	0.56	1.78	1.88	1.22	1	1.22

■ Social/Health

In other countries, the services and budget for frail elders is a subject of political action, so a topic like housing adaptation is in the public debate about priorities, alongside considerations of the desirability of more specialist physicians or another MRI machine. In the U.S., the delivery system provides no time and place at which the management functions for medical and social services come together, not even in local or state politics. At the federal level, these issues are in different agencies, different funding streams, and even different Congressional committees. These worlds have separate conferences, research methods and literature, funding streams, legislative committees, personnel training and incentives, and even different words used in the work. For example, medical providers call frail elders "patients," while the social services world calls them "clients," and in nursing homes, they are "residents."

The elderly person and family often assume that some thoughtful folks have put together a care system that makes sense, but that is not the case. These services have grown up in response to needs and opportunities, with no substantial coordination or planning. In most other countries, eldercare issues come together in a socially sanctioned process: e.g., the county council in Sweden, or the Local Health Integrated Networks in Ontario, Canada.[108,109] But not in the U.S.; we have no locus at which responsibilities for the needs of the frail elderly population come together, or for anyone to set priorities and monitor progress. But for frail elders to thrive, these domains of services must interact and collaborate, and priorities among them need to be set in order to serve the interests of the population. This does not now happen; medical care is so dominant and all other services are so stunted that overuse of medical services is rife and shortcomings in supportive services abound.

This overspending on medical care, slim availability of social and supportive services, and lack of anyone seeing the whole picture or taking responsibility for addressing critical needs yields a bizarre truth: In the U.S., a physician can write a prescription for a very expensive medication that is not likely to work for an elderly patient; but that physician cannot get home-delivered meals for this patient, nor can anyone else. In some parts of the country, waiting lists for Meals on Wheels exceed 4,000 people.[110] Indeed, in my travels I've found cities where the wait is sometimes a year long. Thomas and Mor estimated

---

[108] (Ontario Local Health Integration Network n.d.)

[109] (Government Offices of Sweden n.d.)

[110] Personal communication from Erika Kelly, Chief Advocacy and Government Affairs Officer, Meals on Wheels America, May 18, 2016.

that increasing support for home-delivered meals by 1% would save 1,722 Medicaid beneficiaries from placement in a nursing home.[111]

These striking waiting times are allowed to grow despite the obvious suffering and malnutrition of frail elders and the evidence showing that home-delivered meals can help prevent frail elders from entering nursing homes.[112] On the other hand, Medicare coverage does not generate any wait for a high-cost, low yield drug, test, or treatment. A MediCaring Community can address this distortion by assessing all needs and shifting some resources to address the critical shortcomings of their local system. Efficiency demands that responsibility for particular services be matched with expertise; for example, housing experts should be working on housing, rather than leaving it to physicians and hospital social workers whose only easily accessed option ordinarily is nursing home placement.

The hallmark of frailty in old age is an increasing dependency on others. Medical services are important, of course, but the basics of living often become the elderly person's main concerns: food, clothing, shelter, basic hygiene, socialization and meaningfulness, burdens imposed upon family caregivers, and impoverishment from the costs of purchased services. The well-funded medical care system has been largely blind to these issues, assuming that "someone else" is responsible, but being paid well to pick up the pieces when inadequate attention to these needs generates a medical crisis. The nation did acknowledge the role of long-term supports in passing the Older Americans Act as part of the trio that shaped Medicare and Medicaid fifty years ago.[113] However, the Older Americans Act has been ignored and underfunded and the U.S. has not really confronted or resolved the challenges posed by ever larger numbers of persons needing a great

---

[111] (Thomas and Mor, The Relationship between Older Americans Act Title III State Expenditures and Prevalence of Low-Care Nursing Home Residents 2013)
[112] (Thomas and Mor, Providing More Home-Delivered Meals Is One Way To Keep Older Adults With Low Care Needs Out Of Nursing Homes 2013)
[113] (Older Americans Act of 1965, Public Law 89–73 1965)

deal of help in order to live reasonably well in old age.[114] Instead, we've enabled medical care to provide rescue when things get very bad. The time has come for a more balanced approach that would supplement and monitor social and supportive services, aiming to learn how to provide the optimal array of services to ensure that frail elders can live as comfortably and meaningfully as possible, at an affordable cost to them, their families, and the society at large.

This chapter responds to these key questions:

4.1 What are long-term services and supports (LTSS)?

4.2 What are the roles of family caregivers and direct care workers?

4.3 How is eldercare financed now?

4.4 How will a MediCaring service delivery model integrate LTSS and medical services for frail elderly individuals?

4.5 How will a MediCaring Community integrate LTSS and medical services for the local system?

---

[114] (Parikh, Montgomery and Lynn 2015)

4.1 What are long-term services and supports (LTSS)?

Despite surveys that indicate our overwhelming preference to grow old, live independently, and die in our own homes,[115] we will mostly face old age encumbered by multiple complex health conditions; and we will, at one time or another, need some long-term services and supports. If we hope to stay at home—or, at least, to stay in the community and not in an institution—we will need services that support independence, including home-delivered food, adapted transportation, disability-appropriate and affordable housing, personal care assistance, help to manage finances, and support for voluntary caregivers. We will need health care, to be sure, but we will also need help in order to accomplish everyday activities that we have been used to doing for ourselves when we were simply ordinary independent adults. Some of us will, eventually, need more comprehensive support than can reasonably be provided at home and will need to move into a facility that can provide long-term care services, which might be housing with services on-site, an assisted living facility, or a nursing home.

Consider, for instance, a still-recovering frail elder upon discharge from the hospital. She gets home to a house that has stairs at the front door that she cannot climb (in or out), or bathroom doors too narrow for her wheelchair or walker, and her kitchen stinks from the food left in disarray when the ambulance crew transported her out. Or consider the heart failure patient discharged from the emergency department who must wait 6 months for Meals on Wheels and, in the meantime, can only obtain canned meat and vegetables or fast food laden with salt. Both of these patients need an attentive friend or family member who will help out, but they have no one. These all-too-common situations eventually cause healthcare setbacks, trigger re-hospitalizations, increase suffering, and lead to very high costs.[116] With

---

[115] (Harrell, et al. 2014)
[116] (Seligman, et al. 2014)

coherent planning across spheres of care and influence, and buttressing of LTSS availability, these errors could have been avoided—and elderly people could live better at lower cost.

The services often included as part of LTSS are as follows:

- Care coordination/case management/navigation
- Personal care (baths, toenail cutting, hairdressing, bed changing)
- Homemaker services (cleaning, cooking)
- Home hospice
- Adult day care and day hospital services
- Home-delivered meals or food
- Meals at congregate sites
- Home reconfiguration or renovation (ramps, lighting, grab bars, toilets)
- Caregiver skills education, group support, respite
- Medication management (loading pill dispensers, ensuring access to medications)
- Skilled nursing (wound care, handling special medications or devices)
- Telephone reassurance and monitoring services
- Technologies that promote connectivity
- Emergency and urgent advice and help for non-medical issues
- Equipment rental and exchange
- Adapted transportation, door-to-door
- Help with legal and financial issues
- Investigating potential abuse, fraud, or neglect
- Counseling to improve family dynamics
- Friendly visitors and telephone networks for socialization
- Socialization (calling networks, neighborly check-ins, group activities)

If a person has the good fortune to live in a community that has insisted on ensuring nutrition for all or has been pursuing universal design in all new and remodeled housing, frail elders in that community will have many more options and much more confidence, compared with elderly persons living in a community that has not acted to address these issues.[117] So much of what happens for supporting frail elderly people depends upon community action. No one person can make the food delivery wait list disappear, or train a cadre of aides with skills to deal with dementia, or have a responsive agency to investigate and alleviate neglect or abuse. Indeed, no one nursing home resident or family member can substantially improve the quality of care in a nursing home. These things have to be done for the affected population of frail elders, usually defined by where they live.

When Medicare and Medicaid passed in 1965, the vision of a safe and supported old age required a third component, the Older Americans Act (OAA) , which was to provide an array of services to support elderly people at home. The OAA was not means-tested. It meant to provide federal support to local initiatives that would provide supportive services. OAA funding has generated the national network of Area Agencies on Aging (AAAs) , which must provide referrals to services in their areas and may directly provide services as well.[118] The Administration on Aging (AoA) works in partnership with State and Area Agencies on Aging to provide the Eldercare Locator database, a public database of potentially available services which is available at eldercare.gov.

OAA funding, along with supervision by the federal ACL and coordination by the AAA local entities, and supplemented by state and local initiatives and philanthropic contributions, has generated the "aging services network," a fragile and unofficial patchwork of mostly non-profit charities and businesses providing services in communities nationwide. These agencies take on all sorts of supportive endeavors, from helping elders to file their taxes to finding volunteers to build a

---

[117] (Oosting 2014)

[118] (Administration on Aging, Administration for Community Living, Eldercare Locator n.d.)

wheelchair ramp, and from assessing the home environment for safety to providing respite for exhausted caregivers. Obviously, such a panoply of thinly funded and uncoordinated endeavors can leave some needs unaddressed and others met with inadequate reliability and skill. The OAA funding levels have increased far less than inflation alone and dramatically less than the population growth. Therefore, waiting lists have arisen for most services, and some, like respite for caregivers, only exist in very limited special programs.

The following graph illustrates the growth of the aging population in relation to changes in OAA funding and total Medicare expenditures.

Figure 4.3: Growth of the Aging Population Compared with Changes in OAA Funding and Medicare Spending[119]

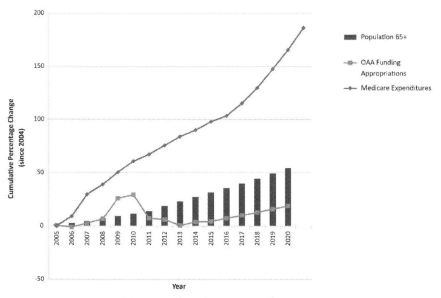

Source: OAA Funding Appropriations: Congressional Research Service; Medicare Expenditures: the Centers for Medicare and Medicaid Services; Population: U.S. Census Bureau. Values have not been adjusted for inflation.

---

[119] Figure 4.3 is based on data presented in N Engl J Med 373;5 (*nejm.org*), Ravi B. Parikh, M.D., M.P.P., Anne Montgomery, M.S., and Joanne Lynn, M.D., The Older Americans Act at 50—Community-Based Care in a Value-Driven Era, July 30, 2015, pp. 399-401. Copyright © 2015 Massachusetts Medical Society. Reprinted with permission. Data source for OAA Funding Appropriations is from: Congressional Research Service; Medicare Expenditures: the Centers for Medicare and Medicaid Services; Population: U.S. Census Bureau. Values have not been adjusted for inflation. Projection for OAA appropriations assumes linear growth at the same rate of FY2015 to FY2016, based on the President's budget.

LTSS discussions usually focus on what are called "concrete services," those that yield specific, observable actions or products. However, elderly people often have a high priority for socialization itself: having someone to listen when a person needs to talk, sharing worries and fears as well as fun, and providing love and affection.[120] Often frail elders find their lives increasingly isolated as spouses and friends become ill and die, driving becomes restricted, and physical limitations make it harder to socialize. The sense of belonging as well as the warmth, nurturing and assistance with information and problem-solving that come with human interaction are all components that contribute to a frail elder's well-being and often are no longer available without some organized community-based supportive services.

4.2 What are the roles of family caregivers and direct care workers?

Family caregivers provide voluntary and unpaid services for frail Medicare beneficiaries. But relying heavily on family caregivers is already difficult, and will become much more so as the numbers of elders needing LTSS doubles in the next quarter century, and the number and availability of family caregivers declines steeply. PBS NewsHour released a telling infographic: "The $234 billion job that goes unpaid," which characterizes the context of family caregiving to older adults. If family caregiving were a federal agency, it would be the fifth largest.[121] An AARP report tallied unpaid caregiving as being worth $470 billion in 2013.[122] In the U.S., family and friends continue to provide most LTSS, providing more than three-quarters of the overall caregiving time for older adults living in the community.[123] The availability of family caregivers is projected to decrease rapidly as the

---

[120] (Hogan, Linden and Najarian 2002)
[121] (Shell 2013)
[122] (Reinhard, et al. 2015)
[123] (Freedman and Spillman 2014)

Boomer generation ages into the years of having a high likelihood of being frail.[124] Not only are families small and dispersed, but also spouses and children of the Boomers generally do not have adequate retirement security for themselves and must keep working if they can, and some will themselves be old enough to have limitations in their capabilities to provide heavy care. Any plan for the future care of frail elderly people is going to have to consider the prospects for making it easier for family members to serve and also for encouraging neighborly volunteering to help with socialization, minor home repairs, and food delivery and preparation.[125,126]

Although caregivers often find the experience of helping others to be a rewarding one, most pay a substantial physical, emotional and financial toll for their effort. Although men increasingly serve as caregivers, most caregivers are midlife and older women. Anyone who takes on substantial volunteer caregiving can compromise their own well-being. For example, those who leave the workforce to care for another adult lose hundreds of thousands of dollars in income, retirement contributions, and Social Security. One estimate calculated that the average sum is $303,880 per person.[127] The work includes the stress of making decisions that have substantial effects on the lives of loved ones, and it includes taking responsibility for intimate and technical services that are ordinarily relegated to persons who are trained and licensed. More than half of family caregivers to persons over age 65 have to provide complex medical care to loved ones– usually, with little or no training as they try to manage medications, clean wounds, change IVs, replace catheters, and more.[128]

Despite their tremendous responsibility for making the plan work, caregivers are seldom integrated into the care plan itself. The

---

[124] (Redfoot, Feinberg and Houser 2013)
[125] (National Care Corps Act of 2015, H.R.2668 2015)
[126] (Caregiver Corps Act of 2014, S.2842 2014)
[127] (MetLife Mature Market Institute 2011)
[128] (Spillman, et al. 2014)

MediCaring approach aims to change that dynamic, by identifying, recognizing, and supporting caregivers, and engaging them in development of a comprehensive care plan with the frail elder they serve. Care teams in MediCaring communities will set out to understand the caregiver's situation and their skills and capacity to provide needed services. Among the services that many communities may come to prioritize will be easier access to respite care, so that family caregivers can have a break and take care of health or personal matters.

The investment in community needs that a MediCaring Community will provide will shape the roles of family and friend caregivers. For example, when a MediCaring Community decides to supplement personal care for frail elders in their own homes with paid caregiving and part-day congregate services, family and friend caregivers will face fewer physically taxing tasks such as bathing and assistance with eating. Freeing up family and friends from some often difficult and contentious daily care demands will allow them to focus on providing affection and life satisfaction activities. Support from others can be important in reducing stress, increasing functioning, mitigating isolation and loneliness, and reducing depression and anxiety.[129] Perceived positive support from family and friends is important to everyone, but especially to a frail elder with limited options.[130] Strong social support helps a frail elder still feel valued and appreciated as a human being. Essentially, social support protects or "buffers" the elder from the stressful vicissitudes of frailty. Furthermore, being in a supportive and well-designed care delivery system would relieve the elder and the family caregiver of the constant anxiety and need to sort out and navigate the uncertain availability and suitability of supportive programs in the area.

Not only will MediCaring Communities provide supports to family caregivers, but the local advocacy that will arise to gather the

---

[129] (Nicholson 2012)
[130] (Potts 1997)

evidence for enhanced investment in caregiver support could be part of a larger effort to generate political action on behalf of family caregiving. Local groups that self-organize and develop agendas will likely converge upon a few key issues and take them to state and federal levels for backing as well as to the MediCaring Community locally. This would be a major step forward for eldercare, since advocacy on behalf of the needs of frail elders has mostly focused on nursing home shortcomings and Medicare coverage rules, rather than on broader issues necessary to ensure reliably high-quality and affordable services.

Providing personal care to millions of frail elders is going to require major changes in society's institutions and expectations. Not only will family and friend caregiving change, but so will the paid personal care workforce. This large cadre of (mostly) women working at low-paying and low-prestige jobs has historically been thoroughly ignored and marginalized by having few career opportunities, and until recently, none of the usual labor protections such as minimum wage, overtime, sick leave, and paid vacations.[131] Yet, the numbers of direct care workers will have to grow dramatically with the rise in the numbers of frail elders and the paucity of family caregivers. Already, the personal care workforce includes more than three million people, more than half of whom are women of color.[132,133] With needs for that workforce set to double in the next dozen years—and requiring training and support in order to offer good-quality, consistent care—social policy must require that these workers earn reasonable wages and benefits and be able to provide for their own retirement and to recover from injuries at work. Recently, the Department of Labor issued its regulatory revision of the companionship exemption, which had previously excluded these workers from the basic labor protections provided by the Fair Labor Standards Act. After being held

---

[131] (Marquand 2015)
[132] (Marquand 2015)
[133] (PHI National 2013)

up by litigation for nearly a year, the Department of Labor began full enforcement of the regulation in January of 2016.[134]

Policymakers have been quite concerned with the risks of fraud and abuse (mainly billing for services not provided) in home care, where direct supervision and monitoring is challenging. Video surveillance and other monitoring and accountability techniques are increasingly available (e.g., video clocking in and out on the internet for each visit made by an aide). These techniques may make concerns for fraud and abuse less prominent over time. The family or an agency could check on the presence and many of the activities of the home health aide to detect non-attendance, troubling interpersonal relationships, and other problems. Then, public attention could focus on recruiting people with helpful skills and attitudes, giving them support and decent wages, and making it possible for people to be proud to be in this line of work.

4.3 How is eldercare financed now?

In October 2014, the New York Times chronicled the story of a frail elderly man who wanted to go home to his apartment in his final months but the incentives and limitations of the delivery system ended up preventing anyone from fulfilling this fervent wish. However, the "system" spent more than $1 million for nursing home, hospital, and emergency services that he, mostly, did not want.[135] Stories like this are commonplace; indeed, so common that people count themselves lucky if the last years of life go well for a family member. Serious illness and disability is now the most common cause of personal bankruptcy, and most long-stay residents in nursing homes have already or will soon "spend down" to the severe impoverishment that is required for Medicaid to pick up the costs of LTSS.[136,137]

---

[134] (Department of Labor n.d.)
[135] (Bernstein 2014)
[136] (Himmelstein, et al. 2009)

Americans turning 65 today will incur an average of $138,000 in LTSS costs, about half of which will be paid out of pocket. Nearly half will not have any LTSS spending at all, while 15.2% will have at least $250,000 in total spending.[138]

Those needing LTSS have about 10% of those costs borne by Medicare, 1/3 by Medicaid, and half by private resources, with smaller amounts from the Veterans Administration, Older Americans Act grants, local revenues, and philanthropy.[139] Most people who are paying for LTSS privately do not have insurance covering these expenses and do not have substantial savings, so they will spend all of their assets on LTSS and health care if they live long enough, and thereby will become eligible for Medicaid.

Until recently, Medicare and Medicaid within any one state would have been nearly standardized programs, with few variations concerning eligibility, coverage, and payment. In contrast, LTSS services had had different and changing eligibility criteria, capacities, coverage, and control. Now, Medicare and Medicaid have also become quite challenging to understand, even within one state. The array of financial arrangements and choices in Medicare alone includes traditional Medicare fee-for-service, capitated managed care, special needs plans including PACE, managed Medicare fee-for-service, integrated Medicare-Medicaid managed care, bundled payments, Accountable Care Organizations, a selection of Medigap plans for co-pays and deductibles, and so on. What was frustration with rigid certainties in the past has turned into fear and chaos for many frail elders and their families.

Medicare mainly pays for rescue care—that is, treatment of new and acutely worsening illnesses, rehabilitation, emergency transportation, and hospitalization. In a major updating in 2003, Medicare started paying for prescription medications, an adaptation to

---

[137] (Mehdizadeh, Nelson and Applebaum 2006)
[138] (Favreault and Dey 2015)
[139] (Favreault and Dey 2015)

the increasing cost of medications and their importance in managing chronic conditions.[140] In 2011 in the Affordable Care Act, Medicare started encouraging proven preventive services by eliminating the co-payment on services like immunizations and cancer screening.[141] More recently, Medicare leadership has announced that they intend to move most beneficiaries and services out of the fee-for-service arena and instead pay for services in a variety of ways that link payment to the value of the services.[142] The last few years have seen remarkable disruptions to usual practices, with many demonstration initiatives and reorganizations of service delivery patterns to reduce hospital use and to try to coordinate care outside the hospital. Nevertheless, Medicare has been only a small contributor to paying for the services associated with frailty, such as supportive care for persons with dementia or movement disorders, institutional long-term care, caregiver support, or even the information infrastructure to provide continuity across settings and time. The $18 billion dollar investment in information technology authorized by the Health Information Technology for Economic and Clinical Health (HITECH) Act, in 2009 supported hospitals and physicians but did not support information technology in, or interoperability with, home health, nursing homes, hospice, or community-based organizations.[143]

About 60% of Medicaid LTSS funding supports elders and younger people with disabilities living in nursing homes, with about 40% supporting persons living in the community.[144] Recent estimates do not separate LTSS spending for older adults and individuals under 65 with disabilities, and older data suggest that progress in shifting to support community living for older adults has been slower.[145]

---

[140] (Medicare Prescription Drug, Improvement, and Modernization Act, P.L. 108-173 2003)
[141] (Patient Protection and Affordable Care Act, P.L. 111-148 2010)
[142] (Burwell 2015)
[143] (HITECH Answers n.d.)
[144] (Eiken, et al. 2015)
[145] (Rowland 2013)

However, the proportion of Medicaid LTSS paying for home and community-based services for the combined population has more than doubled since 1995. That increase will likely continue due to recent programs such as Money Follows the Person[146] and the Balancing Incentive Program,[147] which provide funds to states to assist in rebalancing their Medicaid LTSS spending towards community-based services and away from institutional settings.[148] Most Medicaid reforms until recently focused upon the non-elderly, with Medicaid personnel feeling that their program was secondary to Medicare in most eldercare. However, with the advent of increasing numbers of frail elders unable to provide self-care with no family or families that are unable to fill in, Medicaid faces pressures that could lead states to raise eligibility requirements or otherwise restrict the possibility of providing for all beneficiaries. The integrated care demonstrations, for beneficiaries eligible for Medicaid and Medicare in a dozen states are beginning to address this population directly. In at least nine states (California, Illinois, Massachusetts, Michigan, New York, Ohio, Texas, Virginia, and Washington), the implementations have been on a regional or county basis, which could begin to build the data and practices that allow a geographic focus.[149] These programs are also developing some novel metrics, such as "Percent of participants with care plans within 30 days of initial assessment" and "Number and percent of waiver individuals who have service plans that are adequate and appropriate to their needs and personal goals, as indicated in the assessment." These efforts begin the process of developing metrics that matter in the care of the frail elderly population.[150]

Frail elders and family members have some tough issues to deal with in accepting even obvious needs for personal supportive services,

---

[146] (Centers for Medicare and Medicaid Services, Money Follows the Person n.d.)

[147] (Centers for Medicare and Medicaid Services, Balancing Incentives Program n.d.)

[148] (Eiken, et al. 2015)

[149] (Musumeci 2015)

[150] (Zainulbhai, et al. 2014)

adapted housing, paratransit transportation, and family caregiving—
and then in finding and funding the services. Some of the emotional
challenges require resolving the natural resistance to accepting
irreversibly declining capabilities in a frail older person. Also, however,
programs come and go, waiting lists and delays are common, and
support of family caregiving is often missing, so elders and families
must scramble to patch together some workable arrangement.
Scattered sources of assistance of varying utility have come into
existence. By far the most common source of help is the inventorying
of local supportive services and the associated counseling done by the
Area Agencies on Aging (AAA), which serve every community
throughout the U.S. The Eldercare Locator at 1-800-677-1116 or
www.eldercare.gov provides a directory of AAAs for every part of the
country. Nearly three quarters of AAAs also serve as Aging and
Disability Resource Centers (ADRCs).[151] ADRCs are a collaborative
initiative by CMS and the Administration for Community Living
(ACL) to establish highly accessible entry points into the LTSS system
in communities across the country, and to provide reliable, unbiased
information on public and private LTSS benefits to individuals and
families at all income levels.

In addition, many managed care organizations, hospitals, ACOs,
health plans, insurers, and Medicaid offices provide some sort of
navigator service, variously called care managers, care coordinators and
care navigators. Under current practice, a fragile elder with multiple
chronic conditions may end up with multiple such navigators aiming to
coordinate care and manage illnesses. The impact of these roles is
unclear. Sometimes, the navigating person pulls together a real care
plan, acts as helmsman for the care team, activates the elder and family
to be more confident and assertive, and identifies and is able to initiate
the appropriate services. But in other cases, navigators give conflicting
commands, misunderstand the situation, focus only on pressing for the

---

[151] (National Association of Area Agencies on Aging and Scripps Gerontology Center
2014)

management of one part of the elder's overall situation, or work mainly from a distance with no on-the-ground insight into the personal situation of an elder struggling to cope with a complicated situation and a lack of familiarity with local resources.

4.4 How will a MediCaring service delivery model integrate LTSS and medical services for frail elderly individuals?

The keys to effective integration of LTSS and medical care to achieve trustworthy, comprehensive services lie in the care team and the care plan (see Chapter 2). The care team must function with respect for the skills and commitment of the team members, which will generally require some training for and attention to teamwork. In the recent initiatives to improve care transitions, observers of the initial efforts at teamwork often noted that the hospital clinicians were powerful, assertive, well funded, and sometimes even arrogant, and community-based service providers were so dependent upon hospital referrals that teamwork across institutional boundaries was not possible until some baseline trust, respect, and honesty developed. Of course, the elderly patient and family were usually left out of the care team. Hospitalization of a frail elderly person ordinarily represents the "failure mode" in the chronic care plan. While hospitalization for swift, substantial, and unexpected changes in condition is important, the day-to-day support, prevention, and enablement that are at the heart of a solid, forward-looking care plan should serve to organize timely, appropriate services nearly all of the time. A MediCaring approach to care plan development would enhance the functionality of the team, in part by levelling the power relationships between health care providers and those providing social and supportive services. MediCaring Communities would enable shifting substantial focus and some revenues to where they are needed most.

Sometimes, urgent issues created by crises of housing, nutrition, transportation or family caregiving arise. MediCaring Communities will work with the existing aging network to focus on preventing such crises whenever possible and meeting them effectively when they still occur. Direct care workers can be on standby to cover a caregiver crisis; safe housing can be readily available for emergency placement; short-term funding could meet heat or air conditioning needs; and reliable and safe transportation can be available for necessary appointments and other responses. Planning ahead to address the social determinants of health, to prevent calamities when possible, and to mitigate the effects of the remaining health crises can greatly reduce the challenges they pose.

In the near future, wider use of computer applications that allow shared, rapid communication about available services to those involved in care planning will decrease the challenges of establishing and continually re-establishing criteria for eligibility, wait-lists, quality, and availability. For example, a care team will be able to see various factors that influence care decisions: the currently available rooms, services, consumer reviews, quality metrics, bus stops nearby, specialist nurse or physician availability, pharmacy response time, and dozens of additional elements that are important in deciding the best place for a person to live, temporarily or long-term. Furthermore, as Health Information Exchanges come to maturity, they will start including social and supportive services information. Then, the personal record will include not only diagnoses, medications, test results, and other medical information, but also the fact that the person relies on Meals on Wheels or is awaiting installation of a ramp to be able to get outside on her own.

For many of the practices MediCaring programs will be using, clinical measures and standards are not well settled. The initial care teams will need to have access to literature review, expert consultation, networking with other communities, and reporting of insights and data. From this work will come new standards and metrics and new wisdom in handbooks, toolkits, and textbooks. This process may well require a dozen years to be mature, but early gains will be striking.

4.5 How will a MediCaring Community integrate LTSS and medical services for the local system?

First, the MediCaring Community governance will assure that frail elderly using a MediCaring service initiative will all have a person-driven care plan that includes supportive services as well as medical care. MediCaring does not envision that the local management entity has to be a direct service provider; it could be a manager and a revenue manager for the existing (and gradually improving) array of direct service providers. However, the MediCaring Community will certainly serve as a convener of providers and representatives of consumer interests for the geographic area.

The MediCaring Community will attend to infrastructure issues such as the effectiveness and scope of the Health Information Exchange, which should carry care plans, assessments, and evaluations and make them available to appropriate service providers. To do this, the Health Information Exchange vehicles will have to incorporate information from LTSS and provide information to LTSS providers. This entails careful planning when the work involves entities not covered by the Health Insurance Portability and Accountability Act (HIPAA) and with providers that do not ordinarily work with secure information exchange.[152]

As was explained in Chapter 2, the aggregation of elements of the care plans provides a remarkable tool for estimating service supply and identifying gaps. If the care plans annotate compromises due to service supply or quality, then the MediCaring Community's managers will have that direct evidence as to gaps that are affecting care plans.

The MediCaring Community will manage the ongoing measurement of the system performance, though a contractor or another existing entity could provide the actual data collection and analyses. Those metrics will help forge relationships, since good outcomes for this population routinely entail cooperation among multiple provider types. The key metrics will be in public on dashboards and will be of concern to civic leaders and news media—again, a force for encouraging high performance.

––––––––––––––––––––––––

[152] (Health Insurance Portability and Accountability Act of 1996, P.L. 104-191 1996)

Of course, the MediCaring Community will also be a major convener and a vehicle for building relationships, a function which will be enhanced by having the role of providing some revenues to address serious gaps in the service array. This will engage the public as well as the various provider organizations and will provide a creative disruption in the status quo regarding power and influence.

Neighbors could provide critical support for frail elders' needs, and it seems likely that a MediCaring Community will re-fashion neighborliness to be widely valued and volunteered. Keeping an increasingly frail elderly person in the community might well require having some neighbors who will do minor repairs, bring in food on bad days, check in to talk a bit and be sure things are okay, and notify the right people when something is going wrong. Our historic myth would hold that families should be taking care of their own, but families are small, dispersed, often dysfunctional, and having to work. Already, among women aged 75 and over, almost half (46%) live alone.[153] So, Senior Villages, a possible Caregiver Corps, and other ways to organize neighborliness will be an important component of the eldercare services.[154,155,156]

---

[153] (Administration on Aging, Administration for Community Living, A Profile of Older Americans 2014)
[154] (Village to Village Network n.d.)
[155] (National Care Corps Act of 2015, H.R.2668 2015)
[156] (Caregiver Corps Act of 2014, S.2842 2014)

Core Component #5: Oversight and Improvement by a Community Board

Complex systems cannot function optimally without active monitoring of performance and management toward ongoing improvement, and someone needs to do that work. At present, individual provider and payer organizations manage their medical services under regulation and financing incentives set mostly by state and federal agencies and legislatures. Funding and regulation for LTSS, in contrast, involves the Older Americans Act and the ACL, state and local revenues and agencies, charities, and frail elders and their families (see Chapter 4). A remarkable array of providers is involved in LTSS, including private persons, large organizations, providers in niche services, and providers with broad scopes. Some are also insurers or service brokers. No one at any level is positioned to see how the overall elder care system functions and to detect oversupply, undersupply, and quality problems, and no one even has the responsibility to try to do this.

The issue of management and control will sometimes be contentious and challenging, and there is much to learn in the first few dozen communities willing to pilot the MediCaring Communities approach. We expect these pioneers to implement rather diverse strategies, reflecting the resources and opportunities that their community's history and leadership bring to bear. For present purposes, we are using the term "Community Board" for all of the specific strategies that generate a community's voice to decide evidence-informed priorities for improving elder care in a MediCaring Community.

Holding the financing considerations until the next chapter, this chapter responds to these key questions:

5.1 What characteristics will mark a successful Community Board?

5.2 What capabilities and authorities does the Community Board need to have?

5.3 What sorts of organizational arrangements could anchor the Community Board?

5.4 What would a MediCaring Community monitor to guide decision-making?

5.1. What characteristics will mark a successful Community Board?

An effective MediCaring Community initiative requires that an entity acting in the public interest be monitoring performance and using data to guide improvements in service delivery supply and quality and to ensure efficiency. Who should do that work, and how should they do it? Thinking about this requires stepping back to consider the possible social structures that could engender management functions such as monitoring progress, setting priorities, and implementing improvements. The entity responsible for this work should probably have the following characteristics:

- Be local or regional, so its scope comports with widely understood geo-political boundaries;
- Actively solicit input from the community as to priorities for the care of frail elders;
- Include elders and caregivers in the voting membership;
- Be of a size that is neither overwhelming nor too small to support the endeavor;
- Take responsibility for the well-being of all frail elders in the geographic area, rather than just those with particular funding or providers;
- Be transparent with data and decision-making and accountable to the public for the use of resources;
- Able to build a realistic and inspiring vision of the achievable improved care system;
- Able to build cooperation in the community interest, while respecting the role of competition;
- Monitor service supply, distribution, and quality;
- Monitor the experience of frail elders and their families and the perceptions of the public;
- Provide a forum for considering the data and a decision-making process that sets priorities for improvements;
- Identify opportunities for improvement and see that they are tested and, if successful, sustained;

- Shift attention and resources toward optimal supply, distribution, and quality through influence on law and regulations, capital investment, performance metrics, community development, finance, and workforce enhancement; and,

- Have some widely accepted authority, either by being publicly chartered, by being lodged in a governmental entity, or by representing such a strong coalition that it can act in the public interest without explicit governmental authority.

Why should this capability for monitoring and management be built at the community level? The answer is that people living with serious disabilities in old age come to be tied to their homes. They cannot readily travel even a few hours to get services. What we need at that time in our lives has to be available where we live.

If a community has a cadre of home health aides with skills in serving dementia patients with behavioral challenges, then a family that needs that help will get it. If the community has been attentive to universal design in new construction and renovations, there will be many housing units ready for disabled persons to thrive. If the community has ensured that every elder in need can get home-delivered food, then there is very little malnutrition and hunger. But if the community has not done these kinds of things, then the family and elderly person who need those services will simply be unable to obtain them. No one family can make the system work well if it is not working well for all.

This grounding in the community makes the argument for preferring a community locus for managing the system. Also, a community or its subsets can be small enough for the staff to get to know its resources and flexibilities. A person at the state level cannot know about traffic patterns in bad weather or what pharmacy will deliver after hours; but the person who lives there can know these critical details. Also, part of the workings of a MediCaring Community is to build a commitment to the common good, so that people who forego a costly treatment have the sense that doing so is not only acceptable to them but also benefits their community. People who live in that community should become proud of their shared commitment to a decent last phase of life.

These are also some of the reasons to press for MediCaring Community programs to aim to take substantial responsibility for the well-being of all frail elderly people in their geographic area. Rather than the overlapping patchwork of persons who sign up with one or another health care insurer or who happen to use one or another hospital, a MediCaring Community needs to aim for well-being of the affected persons in the whole population. It will not be enough to provide excellent care to a subset and leave many elderly neighbors facing unreliable services, abandonment, and despair. The MediCaring approach should be the "gold standard" and these services should be available to all frail elders who live in the geographic community. Just as one cannot fix the availability of housing or food for just the persons signed up in a particular health plan, one cannot claim to be responding to the needs of the frail elders in the community if the important services are available only to some of them.

5.2 What capabilities and authorities does the Community Board need to have?

The list of desirable characteristics for a Community Board has been given above. What advice can we give to leaders in communities that aim to establish such a Board? First, organizers will need to consider carefully how to designate their "community." Having well-established boundaries and a clear understanding of how local issues are generally handled will be an advantage. People are more willing to work for the well-being of their own "hometown" than for a set of poorly aligned ZIP codes. In addition, many services are already organized around established geo-political boundaries. This argues for generally using cities and counties. Especially in the initial stages, having a strong community spirit and a tradition of shared governance and community loyalty will help.

The size of the enterprise deserves attention. Generally, very small populations will not have the array of needed services nor the revenues to support monitoring and governance, and very large and populous areas will have too many contentious forces to allow governance to get underway, but both generalizations will have exceptions.

Except for the unusual situation in which a geographic area functions as an island with the health care market area nearly congruent with the geo-political boundaries, there will be mismatches of the boundaries of "community" with the indistinct service area of various service providers in that community. For example, a community with three hospitals might well have at least one that has a substantial proportion of patients from outside the home community. The decision could be to expand the community to include some contiguous areas or to measure quality within the established community but continue to provide services to others. The solution adopted will depend upon local factors, including leadership, funding, and a concern to avoid orphaning nearby areas with sparse populations.

An effort to create excellence in one jurisdiction will attract potential participants from nearby areas. Each community will need to consider how to deal with frail elders who want to join their MediCaring effort but who live outside the covered area. Some MediCaring Communities may, at least at first and when tied to local funding or chartering, simply restrict their geographic scope so they can maximize the effectiveness of their monitoring and system management.

How can the Community Board be vested with appropriate authority? Here are some possibilities. The local government can charter the Board, grant it certain authorities, provide seed funding, require testimony on the adequacy of current service capacity before various arms of government (city councils, zoning boards, etc.). The initial charter can require that the Board have control over reinvestment of some of the MediCaring Community's Medicare savings and that it produce periodic reports as to the progress made in achieving important service improvements for frail elders.

Importantly, the Community Board could be developed by an Area Agency on Aging or a PACE program as a broadening of their existing community advisory board. Government, philanthropy, or their sponsor could provide operational funding and the data needed for monitoring. The Board needs to have an independent voice, so that it can speak out and claim sufficient authority to represent the interests of frail elders, work with the public, and make their insights and decisions very difficult to ignore.

The Community Board needs to represent the interests of frail elders and their family caregivers first and foremost; but it also should attend to the interests of providers, including personal and home care aides. The Board also has to be established in a way that engages and involves locally powerful entities in the community, all while ensuring fairness and openness. The actions of the Board, and the data on which they rely, must be public. At the same time, the identities of individual elderly persons must be kept private unless publicized with knowledgeable consent. This consideration may sometimes make it improper to put data or decisions in public that arose from unusual and identifiable situations. With this exception, the overall patterns of supply and quality and the costs of services require openness to the public. The public should be well informed and should see the process as being trustworthy and valuable. The requirement for openness, along with the pressure to meet more needs, will make it very unlikely that an investor-owned company could operate a MediCaring Community and support its Board, unless they invested through a carefully designed payment plan that limited their return on investment.

5.3 What sorts of organizational arrangements could anchor the Community Board?

The Community Board idea is novel for medical care but builds on an array of governance structures that already serve communities: school boards, neighborhood advisory commissions, and so on. In some communities, an existing medical services provider, such as the county hospital or the only medical care provider in the area is what the community turns to as the organization to remodel and mature into taking on this work. In other settings, a particularly effective Area Agency on Aging, a coalition of providers, or a public-spirited healthcare insurer could take the first steps. PACE programs already have Community Advisory Committees which could broaden and mature to serve this purpose. With the advantage of having established both trustworthiness and administrative procedures, they could invite others to join in a distinct endeavor, with arrangements that do not advantage the initial sponsor. In other communities, the local government or its public health office would be the logical initiator, having the trust, authority, and access to resources to get the work underway. Whoever takes on the organizing will need strong partners in the various provider sectors, as well as the commitment and skill to bring in representatives of the frail elders and their families. We have worked with communities where a very motivated group of citizens are willing to help establish one of these arrangements, even where the government and the providers had little inclination to notice the need before public pressure riveted their attention.

The first dozen pioneering communities willing to implement the MediCaring Communities concept will need to develop a roadmap that can guide success for later communities. Some theoretical touchstones derive from Elinor Ostrom's insights as to how communities can organize to protect "the commons," or their shared stake in a limited resource.[157] Ostrom's "design principles" of how communities can manage a shared pool of limited resources, as adapted for health care, include having clearly defined boundaries for the distribution of shared resources, having principles by which decisions are made, engaging most affected parties in the decision-making, monitoring the process and outcomes, and having the process be recognized and encouraged by state and federal authorities. These principles can help guide construction of social arrangements that enable communities to manage partial funding of gaps and to remedy quality problems. The fundamental concept is to build a self-organized and sustained governance in which all parties are allegiant to the well-being of frail elders.

In most communities, the startup of MediCaring will be smoother and more effective if it builds on a trusted and public-spirited group

---

[157] (Ostrom 1990)

and has strong initial commitments from key medical and social provider stakeholders. The MediCaring Community can grow out of a provider coalition or a citizens' activist group, but it must become a legal entity, on its own or as part of local government or an existing non-profit provider organization, in order to have authority and to be able to manage data and funds responsibly.

5.4 What would a MediCaring Community monitor to guide decision-making?

The Community Board must become an active learning organization, aiming for continuous quality improvement (CQI). The concept of CQI derives from the work of W. Edwards Deming and colleagues, who first showed the potential of guiding reform with rapidly informative statistics and ongoing testing in his quality improvement work with the Japanese automotive industry. Deming exhorted reformers to consider the whole of the system they aim to optimize: "A system consists of components. Any company, any industry, consists of components that are different activities. All the components of the system must contribute to the system, not exist for their individual gains."[158] In general, he said, successful quality improvement efforts require five elements:

- Foster and sustain a culture of change and safety.
- Develop and clarify an understanding of the problem.
- Engage key stakeholders.
- Test change strategies.
- Conduct continuous monitoring of performance and reporting of findings to sustain the change.

In a Medicaring Community, the Community Board will be ultimately responsible for delivering on these requirements, so success

---

[158] (Deming 1994)

requires a comprehensive and appropriate monitoring system that assures timely knowledge of implementation, service supply and quality, and system efficiency. These elements form the nucleus of a community dashboard that will serve to manage and share information about the local system. In addition to tracking progress, the community will need to establish a cost and quality baseline for each important metric, against which to measure system improvement. Monitoring will serve several specific and overlapping goals, as follows:

- Providing rapid and actionable feedback on utilization and costs
- Ensuring quality of care by external standards
  - Functional limitations, symptoms, mortality
  - Medication appropriateness and management
  - Workforce skills and adequate numbers
- Ensuring quality of care from the perspective of the frail elderly person and his or her family
- Assessing supply and distribution of services
- Assessing the effects of elder care and improvements upon the community, including confidence and civic pride.

The strategies to accomplish these ends are numerous, and the ones chosen will depend in part on the availability of timely data in each MediCaring Community. Data will come from the conventional sources of administrative records of claims and payments, questionnaires from the client and/or family representative, and review of the records kept by service providers. These will generate a number of conventional metrics: 30-day readmissions, pressure ulcers, falls, location at the time of death, hospice use, and more. The records will be enriched with comprehensive assessments and care plans, which will anchor new measures of quality and utilization, including adherence to the elderly person's goals and confidence in the care system. The MediCaring Community's Community Board will need to monitor total costs of care, including out-of-pocket costs from patients and families, Medicare, Medicaid, Older Americans Act, local revenues, long-term care insurance, and veteran's benefits.

A characterization of the community's outcome from a sample of case studies that tallied the patient and family experiences and the services provided in the last couple of years before death could help MediCaring Communities estimate baseline performance and costs more accurately. This technique may prove to be an efficient approach for measuring quality of care during the last years of life, and an inexpensive method for auditing the care of all of a community's frail elderly persons. The stories collected would also be very helpful in outreach and education efforts in the community (with family consent to make the information public).

To orient care systems around frail elders' needs and goals, MediCaring Communities need frequent feedback on how frail elderly persons and their families and caregivers experience the delivery system. These elder and family surveys could be very short, consisting of only a few questions, using various rating approaches. They would be designed to generate reports about how often the frail elderly person's situation seemed out of control or frightening, recent health and LTSS use, and how well (global self-rating) the care is meeting their priorities and goals.

Some aspects of care will require assessing the perceptions of key provider stakeholders, e.g., the medical director of the emergency department, emergency transport staff, a funeral director, local hospice leaders, and intervention leaders. The themes and trends in these interviews should illuminate how substantially practices have changed in the community, what shortcomings participants are seeing, and the general level of enthusiasm for ongoing change.

Some events are so distressing that the MediCaring Community should require reporting and investigating them. Major treatment errors and many hospital-acquired problems are already reported to public officials for all patients, and these could be publicly reported separately for a subset of frail elders. Other errors that especially affect this population should be reported and analyzed within a MediCaring Community: e.g., medication errors with harms, falls with injury, failure to follow an explicit and appropriate advance directive, onset of a new stage III or IV pressure ulcer, family caregiver quitting or self-harm, inadequate supply of an important service, and enrollee or caregiver distress with services.

The Community Board will need an appropriate staff and internal and technical support capabilities to manage data and public display quickly and efficiently.

Core Component #6: Financing with Savings from Medicare

Dozens of research projects and small demonstrations and pilot programs have shown that better geriatric medical care for frail elders regularly improves care and saves money. Some examples of effective interventions are illustrated in Table 3.1 on page 57. Despite very promising results in so many innovations, these programs have not spread and often have not even been sustained after the initial grant funding has been used. If these innovations were new pharmaceuticals, they would be "breakthroughs" and major entries in the marketplace; but these are prosaic reorganizations of how to deliver optimal care, and our largely fee-for-service Medicare system has not generally had a way to promote uptake of innovations that will reduce services and thereby reduce revenues to providers.

The lack of attention to efficient improvements in eldercare occurs in the context of evidence of remarkable waste in health care generally. Berwick and Hackbarth in 2012 estimated that at least 20% of health care expenditures were utterly wasted in that they provided no value to the patient.[159] In the last few years, health care policy has implemented novel payment arrangements that aim to deliver higher-quality and more appropriate services to Medicare beneficiaries and thereby create savings, using the strategy of sharing the resulting savings between providers and the Medicare Trust Fund to create financial incentives for providers. Medicare programs providing shared savings include Accountable Care Organizations (ACOs), Bundled Payments for Care Improvement (BPCI), and Independence at Home (IAH). For much longer, capitated Medicare programs such as Medicare Advantage managed care and PACE have been able to create

---

[159] (Berwick and Hackbarth 2012)

and retain savings, whether those savings were used to expand services or to enhance their margins.

This growing use of savings in Medicare services as the financial incentive for reforms in serving frail elders opens the important possibility of assigning a portion of the savings to buttress home and community-based services that would otherwise be unavailable because they are not covered by Medicare or financed in any other way. Improving these supportive services will have a substantial effect in further reducing medical care costs; but even more, they will enhance the experience of advanced illness and disability for elders and their families. The MediCaring Community would take this concept one step further by monitoring and improving frail elder care for the entire community.

Leaving the details of implementation to the next chapter, this chapter responds to these key questions:

6.1 What is the estimated magnitude of savings from more appropriate medical care for frail elders in a MediCaring Community?

6.2 Will more LTSS also yield reductions in the use of medical care?

6.3 How should savings be allocated and what will be the effects?

6.4 How will the MediCaring Community initiative evolve with the increasing numbers of frail elders?

6.1 What is the estimated magnitude of savings from more appropriate medical care for frail elders in a MediCaring Community?

The costs of overuse of medical interventions show up in virtually every effort to optimize care. An overview of the main innovations reported in the literature is in Chapter 3, Table 3.1: Evidence-Based Clinical Improvement Examples, on page 57. As described in Chapter 3, a number of elder care reform programs, such as Independence at Home, PACE, GRACE, and the Veterans' Home-Based Primary Care, have improved quality of life while substantially reducing use of hospitals and nursing homes and lowering costs.

The public often assumes that the waste in medical care is in high-tech interventions, like resuscitation, intensive care units, and transplants. In Medicare, the waste and very low value care is at least as likely to be in thoroughly ordinary care for routine situations, in which the elderly person is given ill-advised diagnostic testing or prevention screening as well as unwanted and often unused treatments. For example, my mother compressed a vertebra when she was 90 years old, probably when picking up a small suitcase. She ended up with two trips to the emergency room to get a diagnosis, multiple imaging studies (bone scan, CT scan, MRI scan, two sets of plain x-rays), a specially manufactured corset which was entirely too large, and an orthopedist who very much wanted to inject her spine to "reinflate" the vertebra (a procedure known as vertebroplasty). The cost of the tests and visits and corset came to about $10,000, and the vertebroplasty would have added at least $20,000 more. The vertebroplasty procedure has been the subject of two randomized controlled research trials (with the control group getting the identical patient experience without the actual injection, so no patients knew whether they got the actual intervention). Both studies showed that the vertebroplasty had no advantage, had some serious but uncommon immediate side effects, and was actually likely to increase the risks of more fractures of neighboring vertebrae.[160,161,162]

What did she need for optimal care? No diagnostic test or medical treatment has been shown to improve upon one ordinary X-ray to confirm the diagnosis and evaluate the spine generally, followed by pain relief and gradual return to function. This requires support by a skilled home care nurse to manage pain medications, encourage re-ambulation, assure nutrition, and arrange homemaker services as needed over the next month or two. All those imaging studies were searching for a cancer, but they could have been done for the tiny percent of elderly patients with vertebral fractures that do not improve as expected, rather than being done immediately; and the corset was just a thousand-dollar error. Optimal care could not have cost more than a few thousand dollars. But every provider got paid for all those extra activities, and they would have made money on the vertebroplasty, too.

A colleague once pointed out: "If we paid religious leaders by the prayer, there would be a lot of prayers said." In Medicare, we still mostly pay "by the service," so we get a lot of services, including those with very low expected value, and sometimes even harmful ones. One might think that managed care would vigorously go after these opportunities for savings; but until recently, their efforts in this regard have been thin, in part because few clinicians recognized frail elders as any different from younger adults, in whom testing for infrequent etiologies might be justifiable. With geriatricized medical care (Core Component #3, page 47), the elderly person and family are clearly placed in a position of control, and the care plan (Core Component #2, page 23) reflects their priorities and goals. In our current climate of overuse, good decision-making and care planning will reliably reduce medical costs.

---

[160] (Buchbinder, et al. 2009)
[161] (Kallmes, et al. 2009)
[162] (Trout, Kallmes and Kaufmann 2006)

To create a full prototype that other communities could look to for guidance, we analyzed how the MediCaring Community model would work in these four diverse geographic areas: Akron, Ohio; a section of Queens, New York; Milwaukie, Oregon (a suburb of Portland); and Williamsburg, Virginia. We researched the range of reported savings in various initiatives and conferred with clinical leaders in each site. From that process, the teams came to consensus as to how much change they could confidently expect to make within 18 months, which we assumed as the start-up period. The major literature sources and the teams' consensus estimates are given in Table 6.1. These estimates, along with Table 6.1, have been published in Milbank Quarterly.[163]

---

[163] (Bernhardt, et al. 2016)

Table 6.1: Estimates of Effects of Implementing MediCaring in Four Communities

Service	Estimates From Published Research and Pilots		Teams' Consensus on Predicted Changes within 18 months
	Estimate	**Notes**	
Inpatient Hospital	-29% to -66%	2009; NY Independence at Home Act[164]	-25%
	-8% to -33%	2012; demonstrations to cut risky hospitalization[165]	
	-10%	2006; resource use among elders receiving acute care[166]	
	-17%	2011; hospital admissions/savings with INTERACT II[167]	
	-18%	2005; two-year GRACE implementation[168]	
	-36%	2011; FFS readmits with Care Transitions Intervention[169]	
	-61%	2012; readmissions after psychosocial counseling[170]	
Outpatient Hospital	7%	2005; two-year GRACE implementation[171]	10%

---

[164] (New York Academy of Medicine 2009)
[165] (Brown, et al. 2012)
[166] (Jayadevappa, et al. 2006)
[167] (J. G. Ouslander, et al. 2011)
[168] (Counsell, et al. 2009)
[169] (Voss, et al. 2011)
[170] (Watkins, Hall and Kring 2012)
[171] (Counsell, et al. 2009)

Service	%	Source	%
Emergency Services	-10% -35% to -59%	2005; two-year GRACE implementation[172] 2009; NY Independence at Home Act[173]	-25%
Primary Care	-1%	2005; two-year GRACE implementation[174]	30%
Professional Specialty Care	-36% -53%	2005; two-year GRACE implementation[175] 2005; hospital-at-home model[176]	-15%
SNF	-15%	2012; cost-containing care transition strategies[177]	-20%
Home Health	20%	2012; cost-containing care transition strategies[178]	10%
Hospice	67%	2013; advance care planning and quality outcomes[179]	10%
Ambulance		Estimates obtained through local survey	-25%
Transportation		Estimates obtained through local survey	100%
Medicaid-covered long-term care	-28% -71% -72%	2013; PACE versus Medicare FFS expenditure[180] 2012; Diversion of nursing home eligible patients to home and community services[181] 2006; interventions for Alzheimer's patients' spouses[182]	-5%

---

[172] (Counsell, et al. 2009)
[173] (New York Academy of Medicine 2009)
[174] (Counsell, et al. 2009)
[175] (Counsell, et al. 2009)
[176] (Leff, Burton, et al. 2005)
[177] (Dobson, et al. 2012)
[178] (Dobson, et al. 2012)
[179] (Bischoff, et al. 2013)
[180] (Wieland, et al. 2013)
[181] (State of Florida Department of Elder Affairs 2012)
[182] (Mittelman, et al. 2006)

We accounted for participants dying or moving away and we used the local estimates of the likely proportion of frail elderly people who would participate. We estimated recruitment, training, equipment, and marketing costs at each site and the development of performance standards and quality metrics jointly. The model was conservative in estimating that the improvements would only be 50% effective in the first year, 90% in the second, and 100% in the third. Overall savings in the steady state would take 20% from baseline medical costs and 5% from institutional long-term care costs. Hospital and skilled nursing facility costs would decrease, but primary care and home care costs would increase. The sites used their local personnel, training, and information technology costs, as well as setting out their best available strategy for implementation, including enrollment.

When we put it all together, the MediCaring implementation yielded a 91% return on investment (ROI) during the startup period and a 249% ROI in the steady state, with the program then projected to be able to sustain operations derived from savings. The total savings over the first three years, as confirmed by an independent actuarial assessment by Ernst & Young, was projected at $57 million, including the costs of developing new methods for quality measurement, implementing program evaluation and quality improvement, setting clinical standards, supporting community organizing, and cross-community collaboration, as well as the on-site start-up costs. After the first three years, the four communities together would generate annual savings of $31 million to use in expanding supportive services, monitoring and managing their system, paying back the startup funds, and sharing with Medicare. A brief summary of the yield at each site is shown in Table 6.2.

Table 6.2: Steady State Estimated Financial Performance for Four MediCaring Communities

	Participants in Year 3	Net Savings in Year 3	PMPM* savings, Year 3
Akron, OH	2,924	$17 million	$328
Williamsburg, VA	1,396	$5 million	$269
Milwaukie, OR	828	$3 million	$291
Queens, NY	1,483	$6 million	$537
Total	6,631	$31 million	

*Per Member Per Month

Clearly, substantial savings are possible. Even in a very low cost Medicare market like Milwaukie, Oregon, the ROI was positive in the second year and the savings were substantial. In a very high-cost area like Queens, savings per person are higher and ROI becomes positive very quickly. The timetable and extent of savings depends on elements of the context and the intervention such as the historical spending pattern, the speed of implementing better geriatric medical care, and the community's trust in the modified care arrangements to encourage participation. However, with our conservative estimates of effectiveness and enrollment, the improved delivery system in a MediCaring Community has substantial opportunity to create Medicare savings.

Recently, the opportunities for savings have been illuminated by the success of companies serving as conveners for bundled payments, such as naviHealth and Remedy Partners. In bundling post-hospital care, naviHealth has posted a report that says that their work saves nearly half of the 10% of Medicare payments that fall into the 90 days after hospitalization.[183,184] The company and the sponsor of the bundle

---

[183] (Linehan and Coberly 2015)

thus earn almost 5% of the entire Medicare budget for their proportion of the beneficiary population, mainly by setting the expectations of patients and families for shorter lengths of stay in skilled nursing or rehabilitation facilities after hospitalization and by channeling some patients into lower cost post-hospital settings. These efficiencies do not worsen health outcomes, and in some cases they actually avoid harms. These strategies do put more burdens on family caregivers or on hired helpers for personal care, but Medicare does not cover these services.

The savings are clearly possible and substantial. Returning these savings to support community services would substantially reduce waiting lists and address gaps in support for frail persons living in the community. The next question is whether an integrated approach with enhanced LTSS would provide further savings, and then whether a MediCaring Community can enable a part of the Medicare savings to be reinvested to optimize eldercare in the community.

6.2 Will more LTSS also yield reductions in the use of medical care?

Ensuring that frail elders have food, shelter, hygiene, and meaningful human contact is certain to enhance their experience of life. Deficiencies in these basic needs are painful, discouraging, and the origin of many issues of ill health. The fear of these deficiencies often yields a crippling anxiety that drives out the possibility of joy and a good quality of life.

But is a frail elderly person who has adequate supports also less expensive? Studies of various interventions in circumstances of deprivation or scarcity indicate that this might well be the case. A study in California showed that poor adults were in the emergency room with hypoglycemia much more often in the last week of each month

---

[184] (Scully 2014)

than in the rest, presumably because they ran out of their monthly allotment of public support for purchasing food ("food stamps").[185] Decedents who had and used long-term care insurance to cover LTSS needs had only 2/3 of the hospitalization costs in their last year, compared with matched decedents who did not have long-term care insurance, and their medication and outpatient costs were lower.[186] One study estimated that every $25/year increase in funding for home-delivered meals per older adult was associated with a 1% decline in nursing home admissions.[187] In people with severe asthma, research establishes that improved housing has a profound effect upon the rates of emergency room use.[188,189,190] The Commonwealth Care Alliance in Massachusetts has a Senior Care Options program for frail elders relying mostly on capitation from Medicare and Medicaid and providing comprehensive services, and it reports cutting hospital days nearly in half and nursing home placements by 2/3.[191]

However, the research is sparse and uneven, and the overall impact probably depends upon how generous the supportive services become. With frail elders, the interaction of the timing of death with the deprivation creates a complicated methodological problem, since persons with such inadequate supports for everyday needs that they die earlier also become less costly. However, a community is likely to be highly motivated to avoid having hunger, exposure, and other seriously adverse human experiences affect anyone in the last years of life. That motivation will probably assure investments to provide these basics, and that might help reduce health care costs. Furthermore, a set of

---

[185] (Seligman, et al. 2014)

[186] (Holland, Evered and Center 2014)

[187] (Thomas and Mor, The Relationship between Older Americans Act Title III State Expenditures and Prevalence of Low-Care Nursing Home Residents 2013)

[188] (Karnick, et al. 2007)

[189] (O'Sullivan, et al. 2012)

[190] (Bhaumik, et al. 2013)

[191] (Meyer 2011)

arrangements that yield confidence in care in old age at current costs helps relieve pressures on other social expenditures, such as schools and infrastructure.

6.3 How should savings be allocated and what will be the effects?

In Medicare programs to date, savings have been used in two ways: to incentivize medical care providers (e.g, IAH and ACOs) and to preserve funds for Medicare (e.g., shared savings in ACOs and BPCI). These are both worthy endeavors, and MediCaring Communities will undoubtedly need to have some savings used in these ways. However, a MediCaring Community also aims to incentivize patients, families, physicians, and everyone else to be prudent and save Medicare funds, in accord with the patient's preferences. Doing so also supplements LTSS and enables measurement and management of the overall eldercare service delivery system. In addition, many programs will have some start-up costs to pay back and some will need reserves in order to take on risks for unanticipated expenditures. This makes for a complicated allocation issue, with legitimate claimants with different agendas and priorities.

In this situation, the Community Board should anticipate what they can and make decisions in the public interest. Considering the well-being of the community is an exercise that will acknowledge such disparate facts as these: that the community needs to develop and retain an excellent workforce, that wait lists for critical services need to be reduced, and that everyone has an interest in preserving Medicare's financial well-being. The public will want both to preserve Medicare funds and also to have their MediCaring Community succeed in serving frail elders well. A best balance of these goals might be to return a share of savings to Medicare only after a few years of getting the initiative underway, but to settle the proportion in initial agreements as the work starts. In many poor communities, the major spur to the economy is funding coming in for health care and social security, which makes another consideration militating for gradual adjustment of that support.[192]

Likewise, if the MediCaring Community endeavor had to borrow start-up funds (including in a social impact bond or pay for success instrument), the agreements made to pay back those loans will need to be honored. Again, the legal agreements set up at the start would do well to allow some time before payback starts so that the elder-centered care initiative can establish itself well in the early years.

The MediCaring Community endeavor will include the medical care systems that are generating the savings, so there will need to be formal agreements as to how to account for revenues and savings and what portion will supplement incomes or otherwise address the proper self-interests of the health care providers. These agreements could take many forms—for example, incentives for productivity or quality or both, income maintenance guarantees, paying off educational loans, recruiting support staff or specialists, or providing medical diagnosis or treatment equipment. The needs of the medical service providers could be handled in the mix with all other community needs or could be a settled aspect of the allocation.

In deciding allocation of savings among service gaps affecting elders, the Community Board (Core Component 5) needs to have a strong voice in setting priorities. The Board should weigh data about the community's supply (both oversupply and undersupply) of services, distribution of availability, and quality concerns. Data about the lived experience of elders and their families will be critically important. The Board itself needs to work on representing community interests well, taking account of public perception, and being able to make decisions and move along.

---

[192] (Berwick and Hackbarth 2012)

Obviously, some regular allocation of the savings will also go to the operations of the services provided in the MediCaring Community: e.g., to gather and analyze data, to hold meetings and handle funds, to advocate policies and educate the public.

Here are some of the key considerations that shape a MediCaring Community revenue management plan:

- Must be auditable and publicly accountable at every stage;
- Must support a trustworthy, reliable set of service providers committed to implementing good care plans;
- Must efficiently support the staff who monitor service supply and quality, manage the data, and provide the administration;
- Must responsibly adhere to the evidence-supported conclusions of the Community Board as to priorities among service needs; and
- Must have a settled and fair method for calculating savings with Medicare.

6.4 How will the MediCaring Community initiative evolve with the increasing numbers of frail elders?

MediCaring will start with some pilot communities and can spread as communities take it up and eventually perhaps, most will. Examining the macroeconomics shows that the economy cannot support decades in which many parts of the country continue spending at the current rate.[193] Civic well-being also will not thrive if we allow decades of generating the anger and frustration that current practices engender.[194] So, the maturing MediCaring Community model would

---

[193] (National Research Council 2012)
[194] (Lynn, Don't Accept Medical Errors as the Standard of Care for Frail Elders 2015)

become the usual way to provide reliable and comprehensive services for frail elders and their families; and for many communities, that reform will carry us through more than a decade of learning and changing expectations.

6.4.1 The eventual need for additional funding for frail elderly people

Reforming services delivery and sharing savings in the manner described here will buy us time and teach us a great deal, and will generate new habits, standards, and understandings. However, tripling the number of frail elders in the first half of this century will leave the U.S. needing more funding for services for frail elders. But if we can restructure care to reduce per capita costs by one-third, which we believe to be possible with MediCaring Communities, the magnitude of the challenge will be reduced. While the timing will differ for different communities, in general the numbers of frail elders needing service will exceed the capacity of current spending at about the time that the Boomer generation hits their years at high risk for frailty, starting in about 2030.

MediCaring doesn't address every aspect of the total financial challenge of an aging population. For example, MediCaring does not address the problem of people not saving for long-term care costs or purchasing long-term care insurance. But, right now the primary choice is "as is" with very high medical costs or "MediCaring Communities" with a lower medical bill and savings. Those savings will not cover all elder social supports for all people, but they will recover the costs of operating MediCaring Communities and meet many of the critical needs in the community.

A prudent person planning for retirement faces two enormous unknown elements: lifespan and long-term care. The costs per person per month with the person's usual retirement lifestyle are fairly predictable, but not how long the person will live. Social Security and many pensions effectively insure for longer survival by continuing a stable monthly payout for as long as the person lives, so if these are the mainstays of support for the elderly person, that particular risk is mitigated for the individual. If, on the other hand, the person has investments and savings as his or her main retirement support, the risks associated with long survival are salient. Of course, many people have little private wealth and will quickly come to rely upon Social Security, low cost housing, and family support.

The financial issues associated with long survival in good health are quickly overshadowed by those associated with long survival in poor health. The average duration of needing someone's help for activities of daily living, for a person at 65 years old, is estimated at 2.5 years for a woman and 1.5 for a man.[195] The costs of in-home half-time support or of residence in a nursing home come to over $100,000 per year, and few people have savings sufficient to keep paying these costs for many years. Paid care at home is more costly than nursing home care, once the person needs paid care more than about 8 hours per day.

Indeed, many Americans wrongly believe that Medicare will take care of most of the costs. However, fewer than half of new retirees have enough money in savings to keep up that rate of spending for one year.[196] The costs of long-term care vary many-fold from one person to the next, and the person who is healthy in mid-life has no way to predict where he or she will fall on the scale of long-term care costs in old age. The response to date has been mainly to avoid the topic entirely, as if we'll somehow deal with it when we must. If we wait, however, the society's options will be much more limited. If we act in the near future, we could have the MediCaring Communities reform mesh with a strategy for longer term financing so that, on average, the nation takes care of itself without major new investments or abandoning frail old people in need.

There still are many ways to deal with long-term disability in old age, but here are some prudent elements. First, it seems impossible for

---

[195] (Favreault and Dey 2015)
[196] (United States Government Accountability Office, Most Households Approaching Retirement Have Low Savings 2015)

people in the middle of life to save enough to cover outlier costs.[197] Somehow, there will need to be a way to cover the costs for those who must live many years with serious disability in old age. This probably ends up having to be a federal backstop that provides coverage after a substantial period of front-end coverage in savings or insurance.[198,199] In addition, a federal involvement can include a reallocation function to diminish the effects of disparities among regions of the country in wealth, prevalence of frail elders, and history of health care utilization.

At exactly what point to start coverage and whether that threshold should be the same for everyone or adjusted for wealth or income are debatable points, but the principle that the long-term care risks must have a backstop in order to enable citizens to be prudent planners is a strong one. At present, the backstop is to spend down to Medicaid and be abjectly poor and abjectly subject to the constraints of your state's program. Without savings and income, some are relying on Medicaid for their first long-term care costs while others will pay for their own services for years before spending down. If the backstop were reliable and made sense, avoiding utter impoverishment might prove to be enough of a motivation to seek to provide for oneself well enough to cover costs at least up to that threshold.

If, for example, the threshold for outlier coverage were set for the average American at the equivalent of two years of full time supportive care (at home or in an institution), then the challenge for the individual becomes bracketed at a total risk of about $200,000 ($100,000 per year for two years). That still is a challenge, and many people won't be able to save that in a lifetime, but with that as the upper bound, purchasing long-term care insurance in reasonably sized pools becomes quite plausible. Half of the people at risk will need no pay-out at all. The long-term care insurance market has been quite limited, for an array of reasons. However, having a federal stop-loss for individual coverage

---

[197] (Favreault, Gleckman and Johnson 2015)
[198] (Favreault, Gleckman and Johnson 2015)
[199] (Hayes, et al. 2016)

would make it possible to field a wide variety of appealing options. Some could take into account the commitments of family to provide a certain level of care (if they are still alive and capable). Some could blend long-term care insurance with other products, such as annuities. Some might test conditioning premiums on preferences for treatments and availability of support at home. If buying long-term care insurance became a standard part of the benefits package for workers, and a reasonable variety of products were offered at fair rates, many more people would undertake a combination of purchasing the coverage and saving current income in order to ensure that they are not impoverished by the usual range of long-term care needs.

With success in hand from experience with MediCaring Communities in the next decade, the funding for MediCaring Community services would gradually shift toward these private sources and the stop-loss federal insurance for very prolonged long-term care, but the clinical service delivery would be unchanged and the system would stay affordable, for individuals and communities.

6.4.2 The easing of pressures for building hospitals and nursing homes

In the average community, the onset of MediCaring and the rise in the affected population will just about balance, thereby averting what otherwise would have been a severe pressure to increase the current supply of hospital and nursing home beds. Rather than having to deal with these substantial capital investments, communities can focus on establishing the patterns that support frail elders at home longer and with more attention to frugality. On the other hand, the rising numbers of frail elders means that current supply of facilities and services generally will not need to be mothballed, even with a MediCaring approach. The increasing numbers will balance the reduced utilization per capita for a while, on average.

6.4.3 Equity across communities

Public spending on Medicare and Medicaid varies a great deal across communities, yielding very different contexts for financing at the start. As is evident in Table 6.2 on page 111, the Per Member Per

Month (PMPM) savings prospects in Milwaukie, OR, and Williamsburg, VA, are dramatically lower than in Queens, NY. This mirrors the high per capita Medicare costs in New York City and the much lower average expenditures in rural Virginia and in Oregon, as well as the substantially more generous Medicaid support in New York.[200]

These differences have long and complicated histories and the pattern of expenditures has generated networks of supporting behaviors in the communities. Nevertheless, with MediCaring Communities depending upon the savings from Medicare, they may soon feel quite unfair. Sometime during the evolution of standards for MediCaring Communities, this inequity of opportunity for Medicare savings is likely to deserve close scrutiny and probably some redress.

---

[200] (The Dartmouth Atlas of Health Care 2016)

Chapter 7: Implementation: Start with PACE

Do you want your community to be a MediCaring Community? Of course you do. Virtually everyone agrees that this is what they want for themselves and for their loved ones. But nearly everyone then says, "But what about *X*?" They fill in the blank with some element of reform that seems to be overwhelmingly unlikely to change. What about the power of the hospitals, doctors, drug companies, and insurance companies that would risk losing income and influence if supportive community services were taken to be important? What about the increased investment in personal care, housing, and food— won't that take away from medical providers? Aren't these social services a "black hole" of need that has no boundaries and will swallow up budgets? What about generating that new layer of governance that watches over the elder care system and makes strategic investments— who will allow that to happen?

One would not undertake a major reform like this if there were easy and appealing options, or if things were working out fairly well as they are. Lewis and Clark would not have headed to the Pacific if there had been an armchair way to figure out what the territory west of the Mississippi held. As a society, we are in the same position regarding elder care. We know that there will be a very large number of frail elderly persons needing a great deal of personal care and a substantial array of services, with the largest increase being in the 2030's. We know that our current temporary illusion of sufficiency already entails a great deal of unnecessary suffering on the part of elders and their caregivers and that the costs already greatly stress families and the national economy. If we do nothing much to improve the situation, we will have to learn to turn a blind eye to an abandonment of many elderly people or to endure a set of serious harms to the economy. We must find a way to care for one another more reliably and with fewer burdens on families and society generally. MediCaring Communities offers the way to do just that. But it won't be easy; it will require the spirit of exploration from the tradition of Lewis and Clark.

Starting with expanding PACE programs offers a very appealing way to establish the first MediCaring Communities, and this chapter will characterize that path. PACE is one of the improvement models we included in Table 3.1 on page 57.

This chapter deals with many of the issues attending a practical implementation of MediCaring Communities, specifically:

7.1 How should we start implementing a MediCaring Communities model? Answer: PACE!

7.2 Which communities should become the first MediCaring Communities?

7.3 What will CMS leadership need to do to make it possible to implement MediCaring Communities?

7.4 What strategies other than PACE can generate a MediCaring Community?

7.5 What could other stakeholders do to help a demonstration of MediCaring Communities to succeed?

7.6 Could social impact bonds or "pay for success" models help with the initial financing?

7.7 After the first set of PACE expansion initiatives, how might MediCaring Communities develop?

7.1 How should we start implementing a MediCaring Communities model? Answer: PACE!

7.1.1. Overview of the PACE Model

PACE (Program of All-Inclusive Care for the Elderly) has an outstanding reputation among beneficiaries, their caregivers, and other stakeholders such as state and federal policy makers. PACE programs receive approval to serve enrollees living within a specific geographic area. PACE assumes broad responsibility for a comprehensive array of services (note: "all-inclusive" in the title) including primary care, hospitalization, and LTSS for their enrolled population, all without co-pays or deductibles. Nearly all PACE enrollees have Medicare and Medicaid capitation, though a few have only Medicaid and even fewer have only Medicare and pay the Medicaid PMPM on their own. PACE programs must operate a physical center for day activities and clinical services and must provide transportation.

Evidence for the effectiveness and cost-efficiency of the PACE model is variable, though the program is widely admired for its comprehensiveness and client satisfaction.[201] Other than generating an operating reserve as a risk-bearing entity, PACE programs are not intended to reduce overall spending. Rather, PACE aims to support substantially disabled people in the community and reduce the need for nursing homes. Savings on medical care buttress operations and services, and nearly all PACE programs are organized as non-profit entities.

Since becoming a permanent program in 1997, PACE has expanded slowly to 116 programs serving almost 35,000 beneficiaries in 32 states.[202,203] Expansion has been limited by an array of statutory

---

[201] (Ghosh, Orfield and Schmitz 2014)

[202] (National PACE Association n.d.)

[203] (National PACE Association, PACE Census and Capitation Rate Information 2015)

and regulatory requirements. Most obviously, PACE enrollment is limited to persons who are 55 years old or older and meet the nursing home level of care in their state but are living in the community without PACE supports at least long enough for what is often a month-long assessment process. Therefore, a hospitalized frail elderly person who wants to use PACE has to go home, at just the time when health is least stable, and go through the admissions process, and then wait until the start of the next month to be enrolled in PACE. Since that person can go directly to a nursing home and the nursing home will be paid retroactively when all the paperwork catches up, the path of least resistance is often just to use the nursing home option.

The initial assessment for PACE enrollment includes face-to-face assessments with at least these eight members of the IDT: the primary care physician, registered nurse, master's level social worker, physical therapist, occupational therapist, home care coordinator, dietitian, and recreational therapist or activity coordinator.[204] The core team can call on others (e.g., dentist, audiology, speech-language pathology) as needed to join in the initial assessment. From the perspective of many frail elderly persons and their families, this can be overwhelming in terms of intrusiveness, time requirement, unfamiliar people, and delay—all for a program which is still unfamiliar.

Frail elders who are not yet impoverished enough to qualify for Medicaid face another difficult hurdle. They must pay the same rate as Medicaid pays for the LTSS components of all-inclusive care that Medicare does not cover. That monthly cost is set at a blended rate to cover the whole range of services, from occasional use of the PACE center to nursing home care, so the fee is usually more than $3000 per person per month. At the time when the elderly person with Medicare-only insurance would most benefit from the coordination and support provided by PACE, the person is not yet using services costing more than $3000 per month, and the elderly person and his or her family

---

[204] (Centers for Medicare and Medicaid Services, Regulations and Guidance Manuals. Programs of All-Inclusive Care for the Elderly (PACE) Rev. 2 2011)

think it is an unreasonable fee. Indeed, they often believe that the elder will die before needing that much service. At a later point when the arrangements for staying at home are falling apart and nursing home care or extensive home care seems likely, the fee suddenly seems reasonable to the elder and family, but not to the PACE program. The upshot is that very few persons who have Medicare but still are not poor enough for Medicaid have signed up for PACE.

For many years, PACE enrollees had to give up their regular physician and come to the day care center at least a few days each week. Many people are loath to give up their physician and change to one they do not yet trust who is hired by a program they do not yet trust; and many also do not want or could not physically manage attendance at the PACE center. CMS now can waive these restrictions, but the PACE program has to undertake to have them waived and many physicians and social workers outside of PACE do not know of the added flexibility after it is granted, so they don't think to refer appropriate patients.

PACE also requires a substantial infrastructure, including the capital investment in a PACE center and clinical site, the data and management for managed Medicare, the data and management for managed LTSS, the acceptance of substantial downside risk, and the liabilities of transportation and activities with a large number of elderly persons with serious physical and mental handicaps. The federal regulations require a one-month operating reserve, and prudence requires building a substantial reserve or having substantial reinsurance to cover unusually expensive medical costs.

An estimated 12% of Medicare beneficiaries over 65 years old are also eligible for Medicaid.[205] The remaining 88% (whom we call "pre-duals") use their personal assets to obtain essential social services and supports and to pay out-of-pocket medical costs or insurance to cover co-insurance and deductibles. They will become eligible for Medicaid if

---

[205] (MedPAC and MACPAC 2015)

they live with high care needs longer than their savings and income can support. They will spend down more rapidly if their services are badly managed and poorly coordinated.

7.1.2. How PACE can expand to lead a MediCaring Community

In November 2015, Congress provided an opportunity to take the straightjackets off PACE. Since PACE was Congressionally established and CMS had been given little authority to test innovations in PACE, and since PACE had been left out of the Affordable Care Act authorization for the Center for Medicare and Medicaid Innovation (CMMI), PACE has always been quite constrained in undertaking anything more novel than PACE itself. The PACE Innovation Act in November 2015 put innovations with PACE under CMMI authority, so CMMI now has broad authority to shape and fund innovations in the PACE model.[206] CMMI can use this authority in a variety of ways. If CMMI allows this, PACE programs could test expanding to serve two additional categories of frail elderly people: (1) persons who are frail but not yet disabled enough to meet their state's Medicaid definition of a nursing home level of care (with or without Medicaid or Medicare coverage), and (2) persons who are still paying for their own LTSS services because they are not yet poor enough for Medicaid. The first group can be called the "at risk" population since they are at risk of progressing to a nursing home level of care. The second group can be called the "pre-dual" population, since they have Medicare coverage and will end up with Medicaid coverage also if they spend down their assets and income to the Medicaid threshold.

As PACE grows to take on these new populations in the defined geographic area, the program would also take on responsibility for monitoring and improving the eldercare services for the community, including persons not enrolled in PACE. We refer to this modification of the PACE model as a PACE expansion program. PACE expansion programs would offer a comprehensive model of care to frail elderly

---

[206] (PACE Innovation Act, P.L. 114-85 2015)

people, without regard to their insurance coverage and whether or not they are disabled enough to qualify for a Medicaid nursing home level of care.

The key elements in the PACE expansion model are these:

- Maintain the multidisciplinary approach with comprehensive elder-driven care planning that is a hallmark of PACE.

- Enable enrollment of persons who are living with disabilities and fragile health associated with aging and who live in the geographic community, but who still have more income and assets than the Medicaid threshold.

- Provide a more flexible set of services that responds to varying needs with a set of private payment levels that makes enrollment affordable to many more people in need of PACE services.

- Meet the otherwise unmet priority needs of the community's frail elderly by investing some of the savings from more prudent use of Medicare funds in community-based services.

- Measure progress, ensure sustainability, and package the model for replication in other communities.

We expect the population who enroll in this flexible PACE expansion model will be comprised primarily of Medicare-only beneficiaries, many of whom also have Medigap to cover deductibles and co-insurance. Few will have long-term care insurance, with the majority therefore being at risk of spending down to Medicaid if they live a long time with substantial medical and LTSS needs.

In traditional PACE, virtually all enrollees are already dual eligible, either because they have been poor for a long time, or because they have been impoverished by the costs of serious illness (for the beneficiary or for a spouse). A few people are not eligible for Medicare, having not worked the required time or not having disability wait time or age qualifications, and each state has a rate for Medicaid-only PACE participants. A very few people in PACE now have only Medicare insurance and not Medicaid, and these elders must buy in at the Medicaid rate. In the PACE expansion program, one of the goals is to enroll persons still capable of paying for many of their supportive care services and to use the program to slow their rate of spend-down to Medicaid by providing more appropriate services aligned with a practical and comprehensive care plan. The opportunities for PACE expansion are illustrated in Table 7.1.

Table 7.1: The PACE Expansion Population: For Frail Elders >55 years old			
	Medicare only	**Dual Eligible**	**Medicaid only**
Elder needs Nursing Home Level of Care	**Expansion** Possible but rare in current PACE	Current PACE	Current PACE Small numbers
Elder does not need Nursing Home Level of Care	**Expansion**	**Expansion**	**Expansion**

7.1.3. Services and Pricing for LTSS in PACE Expansion, 55 years old and older

Payment for the expanded PACE model will be a combination of Medicare, Medicaid, and private payment. Medicare would continue paying the appropriate Medicare Advantage rate as traditionally modified for frailty in PACE. The additional services of PACE could be offered to the Medicare-only clients as a series of tiered packages paid on a PMPM basis. The following are examples of possible tiers:

- **Tier 0:** An introductory package that provides assessment, care planning, and navigation for a small fee and does not require enrolling in PACE. If the person does not enroll, the fee could be paid by Medicare with a new payment code or by the frail elderly person or his or her family. Tier 0 functions both to set things right for the elderly person and to introduce them to PACE. If the elderly person enrolls in PACE, then the PACE program will cover the costs of this assessment, as in traditional PACE.

- **Tier 1:** A basic package of routine and stand-by services: Periodic assessment, care planning, referral and navigation, patient activation and education, caregiver training and support, workforce recruitment and education, medication management and access, short-term or occasional day care, adapted transportation, short-term caregiver respite, and 24/7 on-call assistance (with the beneficiary's care plan in hand).

- **Tier 2:** All of the above plus regular personal care services up to 45 hours per week or regular day care and transportation.

- **Tier 3:** All of the above plus personal care of more than 45 hours per week or long-term nursing home placement.

Tier 2 may need to be split in various ways, or to have some services that are "add on" if needed. Perhaps this would apply to substantial dental needs or needs for especially expensive hearing aids. The exact contents of each tier and the pricing for each will need to be worked out with examples and experience. However, clearly, Tier 0 will incur only a small charge, Tier 1 will be quite affordable, and Tier 3 will be just as expensive as it really is to provide this level of support—often $10,000 per month. The program, the elderly person, and the family will have strong incentives to stretch to avoid Tier 3 costs, which is a good alignment of incentives with the community interest. The comprehensive PACE program and its care planning and coordination will also help to reduce the rate of spend-down to Medicaid among people who enroll as Medicare-only patients.

Depending upon the frequency of Medicaid beneficiaries enrolling before being nursing home eligible, and of Medicare-only beneficiaries spending down long after enrollment, Medicaid may need to develop new payment rates for these new situations.

Certain details of operations have been worked out for traditional PACE, for example, regarding the interface with hospice, Part D medication coverage, long-term care insurance, and disenrollment for cause. These details seem to be generally appropriate for PACE expansion populations and constitute another reason that building MediCaring Communities on a PACE base is appealing.

7.1.4. Quality Measures and Beneficiary Protections

The quality measures that CMS is now implementing for PACE programs are quite limited, focusing on falls, pressure ulcers and readmissions. While these tally certain adverse events in a beneficiary's life, they do not begin to reflect the special character of PACE and the reason that beneficiaries would want their services. CMS has convened a Technical Expert Panel to frame and suggest new quality measures for PACE. CMS or the initial group of PACE expansion programs will have to address the current shortcomings by developing additional measures of quality, both for PACE expansion enrollees and for the frail elderly population in the area, since this PACE expansion will take a true population health approach. PACE expansion programs could try out new metrics that focus on the dimensions of quality that are important to frail elderly patients and families—e.g., confidence in the care system, preparation for the likely course, comfortable dying, reduced caregiver strain, and lower out-of-pocket costs and total care costs.

Since nearly all traditional PACE participants have had no substantial assets beyond their PACE capitations, the negotiated care plan has been the arbiter of services supplied. The dynamics of care planning with populations that still have their own resources and can purchase extra services outside the PACE care plan will require some standard-setting and monitoring.

As with virtually all Medicare innovations, beneficiaries would be free to leave the expanded PACE program service delivery at any time, returning to traditional Medicare or their prior Medicare Advantage plan and, if qualified, to whatever Medicaid program is standard for this beneficiary. The PACE program would have an appeals and grievance process, as it does now, and recourse to the usual beneficiary protection appeals that Medicare and Medicaid provide.

7.1.5. The Expanded PACE Program as a MediCaring Community

With an expanded PACE program, many frail, disabled, and ill Medicare-only beneficiaries could receive the considerable benefits of longitudinal care planning and well-coordinated LTSS without delays and at an affordable cost. Medicare would continue paying the relevant Medicare capitation rate. More appropriately tailored medical interventions would generate savings that the program would use to fund additional LTSS services, thereby supporting highly integrated comprehensive services that would benefit the entire community, as well as providing a focus for monitoring and management of system performance.

The population health management function requires (1) implementation of improved metrics for quality dashboards that reflect patient/family experience and that can be used across the geographic area in order to inform planning, and (2) creation of a trustworthy process for setting priorities for the community's eldercare services.

Current PACE programs have Participant Advisory Committees and must have PACE participant or family representation on their governing boards. The expanded PACE program for frail elders can enhance their existing Advisory Committee to take on the population health monitoring and responsibility for the well-being of frail elders in the geographic area (Core Component #5, page 91). PACE programs can also partner with other organizations, such as local Area Agencies on Aging, to guide the community's progress in efforts aimed at improving the local LTSS delivery system.

7.1.6. How to Implement PACE Expansion for Frail Elders

- Identify states that are willing to expand current PACE programs to serve the PACE expansion populations in a geographically defined community. Enrollment would focus on adults >55 years old who are living with frailty or advanced, complex illness.

- Identify PACE programs and their communities that are eager to test the MediCaring Communities approach to PACE expansion.
- Develop and refine payment approaches, such as a tiered PMPM matched with bundles of services, which would support enrollment of the Medicare-only pre-duals population.
- Develop a community quality performance dashboard with public reporting of quality metrics and goals.
- Gain cooperation with CMS/CMMI in moving ahead

7.2 Which communities should become the first MediCaring Communities?

In the first pilots, only communities with some advantages should implement MediCaring Communities models. The endeavor will have challenges and risks that care patterns will drift back to current dysfunctions. Successful implementation will require a great deal of attention, collaboration, and trust on the part of leaders in the communities, and those are easily disrupted. Therefore, we should start with communities that seem more likely than most to succeed.

What characteristics are likely to predict success?

- *First*, the community should have a tradition of cooperation in the public interest: e.g., generating standardized forms for information transfer at hospital discharge, working together for child health or other social challenges, or raising money for community projects. Communities with factions that dislike or distrust one another would seem to have undue challenges in building the Community Board, referring likely elders to PACE, or supporting the priorities for reinvestment of savings.
- *Second*, the community should have reasonably natural boundaries, so nearly all people already know if they are part of that community or not. The boundaries can be features of the natural topography, or geo-political boundaries, or long-

standing loyalties; but having the market areas of providers match up with the population of concern and the political divisions helps align public investments with private activities. Having most of the medical services provided in the defined community by providers located in that community creates the opportunity for a relatively closed system that does not lose opportunities as does a larger or more overlapping marketplace. In a community where 90% of services to frail elders in the community are provided within the community, the reforms fuel savings that enable community investments. In a community where only 45% of services to that community's frail elders are within that community, the effectiveness of reforms will be attenuated when the elder is getting services outside the community, and savings will be limited by the behaviors of people who are not invested in the community's success.

- *Third*, the community needs to have leaders willing to put their shoulders to the wheel, willing to encounter some adversity, and willing to pursue the vision of good elder care at a sustainable cost despite not knowing all the hazards and challenges along the way. Those leaders can be laypersons, politicians, clinicians, business executives, or anyone else in a position of influence, and ideally the group of leaders willing to undertake the journey will have come from various backgrounds.

We are finding many communities that would be good candidates. Some have citizens' groups that have seen how elderly people are living in their communities now and they see the degradation of even that inadequate level of support as the numbers rise. Some face remarkable short-term increases in the numbers and proportion of frail elders, due to historical and current migration patterns for work and retirement. Some have a health plan or provider with leadership that is fed up with the routine of mismanagement of the issues facing frail elders, often because of experience with a loved one. Professional pride demands that they take steps to improve performance. PACE programs already have a geographic scope and have learned to work with their community's other providers and their civic leaders. So, existing PACE programs in communities with attractive features can take on the initial pilots.

7.3 What will CMS need to do to make it possible to implement MediCaring Communities?

Quite simply, Medicare leaders, or the Congress that can direct CMS to take an action, have to enable the first group of communities with good PACE programs interested in expanding PACE on the MediCaring Communities model to get underway. That is the essential element.

Calculating the Medicare and Medicaid payment rates will require some initial and repeated attention in order to estimate the costs in "usual" care, which is an uneven and often imprecise standard. Whether to cap or reinsure for outlier individual costs, whether to work from a historic baseline or to build in frequent updating, and how to deal with the overlap of other innovations in service delivery and finance will require specification. The negotiation between willing community leaders, CMS, and state Medicaid offices, working in the public interest will yield adequate resolutions.

Another critical element is the current drive for sharing the savings with the Medicare Trust Fund. In most cases, the savings shared with the program have been perceived to be incentives to the professional providers, not an investment in ongoing improvement activities or in the well-being of the public served. This framing is obviously out of step with a plan to expand PACE and build a MediCaring Community. The early sharing of savings that is required of ACOs and BPCI conveners is not optimal for supporting the MediCaring Community pilots. The new model has startup risks and costs. Rather than taking back the savings quickly, CMS should encourage the ongoing investment in reform and in meeting initial expenses. In order to learn to provide efficient and effective services to frail elderly people in communities as quickly as possible, we recommend leaving the savings with the programs for the first five years and then reconsidering on the basis of evidence.

In addition to setting payment rates, Medicare should waive certain of their current regulations, especially those that make it time-consuming and burdensome to enroll in PACE. The current quality measures need to align with what is special in PACE.

7.4 What strategies other than PACE can generate a MediCaring Community?

Any payment arrangement that will leave savings with an entity that can invest in community services is one that can anchor a MediCaring Community, with adjustments in regulations and patterns of care. PACE is the most appealing, because PACE programs already have so many of the key elements in hand. Traditional Medicare fee-for-service is unable to generate a MediCaring Community delivery and financing arrangement, because this payment pattern cannot generate revenues through savings.

An ACO could decide to sponsor a MediCaring Community by accounting for frail elders in a defined geographic area separately from their overall business and establishing an integrated clinical and LTSS delivery system in that community. The savings harvested from avoiding low-value care would be diminished by the share that goes to Medicare and by whatever was retained by the sponsoring ACO. Savings (or cost overruns) are calculated long after the fact, so the delay in having savings to work with will require more initial investment in start-up costs. The ACO clinical services would need to implement good geriatric practices, including for frail elders to have adequate care plans. The usual ACO has little track record to build upon for constructing a Community Board and for collaboration with LTSS providers, but their communities might have strengths in these areas. ACOs also have substantial barriers to establishing dominance in an area and quality metrics that are not aligned with the priorities of frail elders, so both of these would need accommodation by CMS. Finally, ACOs often have quite limited expertise in geriatric medical care and would need to build strong provider teams quickly.

A managed care organization (MCO) likewise could sponsor a MediCaring Community, parallel to the ACO strategy above. The

MCO would collect its PMPM and savings are the profits in hand. The challenges in developing clinical expertise, care plans, connections with LTSS providers, and a Community Board will be fairly similar to the ACO issues outlined above. MCOs also face the challenges of the star rating system for quality. Excellent frail elder care will mean not complying with many of the standard quality metrics, like tight control of diabetes and hypertension and screenings for cancer. This will bring down the MCO star rating, which has a substantial impact upon their Medicare reimbursement. Also, MCOs are not allowed to offer some services to only some patients; they must offer the same package to all beneficiaries. So an MCO cannot offer a MediCaring Community package in one area and not in others without a waiver of this requirement.

Other platforms are plausible but more of a stretch—IAH, hospice, and even bundled payments for a year-long or life-long bundle for persons with complex illness or frailty. These other approaches have more challenges initially than working first with expanded PACE programs. PACE has more of the essential elements in hand and much of the appropriate philosophy. PACE has a good reputation to build on, and most of the programs rooted in their communities. Table 7.2 below gives an overview of the comparison among potential delivery and payment platforms and makes it evident why PACE expansion is so appealing.

Table 7.2: Attributes of Potential Sponsors of a MediCaring Community

	PACE	ACO	MCO	IAH	Hospice
Targets frail elders	Only	No	No	Sicker Subset	Varying but has Modest Overlap
Geriatric expertise and inter-disciplinary teams	High	Low	Low	High	Varies
LTSS expertise	High	Low	Low	Moderate	Low
Care plans & on-call	High	Low	Low	High	High
Rapid implementer	High	Low	Low	Low	Low
Community Board	High	Low	Low	Low	Low
LTSS integration within a budget	High	Low	Low	Low	Low

7.5 What could other stakeholders do to help a demonstration of MediCaring Communities to succeed?

Many parties could take a variety of actions to help the first MediCaring Communities to succeed. Here is a preliminary list with the entity that could take action and the action desired:

- CMS could provide startup funding through their Center for Medicare and Medicaid Innovation.

- CMS could waive a set of regulations that are well-known to make it unduly complicated to manage a population living with serious illnesses: waive the 3-day hospitalization requirement for eligibility for skilled nursing facility care; waive the requirement to be homebound in order to have home care services; and allow nurse practitioners (where allowed by state law) to authorize any level of care that a physician now must authorize, including generating care plans.

- The Agency for Healthcare Research and Quality (AHRQ), or CMS could fund the development of suitable quality measures and could assure that CMS or a contractor would take on the responsibilities of stewardship for the resulting measures.

- AHRQ or CMS could fund a professional group (like the American Geriatrics Society) to develop evidence-informed clinical standards for this population.

- CMS could provide much of the ongoing data needed for management as part of a plan for evaluating the performance and estimating the savings.

- CMS could work with consumer representative groups to ensure that beneficiaries have adequate protection for their well-being and the privacy of their records.

- CMS, AHRQ, and the Centers for Disease Control and Prevention (CDC) could fund development of a set of population-based measures, including management tools based on the community dashboard and the aggregation of community care plans, that would inform the Community Board as to priorities and progress.

- The Patient-Centered Outcomes Research Institute (PCORI) or another party could take steps to ensure that elderly persons and their surrogates have good information about their choices.

- CMS, ACL, CDC, or AHRQ could contract to develop materials to enable community members to serve effectively on the Community Boards (as CDC has done for tobacco control).

- The state Medicaid programs should collaborate to discern the effects upon their beneficiaries and budgets.

- Cities, counties, and states could set up conditions that make it easier to move toward efficient services when they need to be delivered to homes by enabling geographic concentration of providers.

7.6 Could social impact bonds or "pay for success" models help with the initial financing?

If CMS or another entity funds the quality measure development and evaluations of the overall initiative and provides technical support (including support for collaboration), then the start-up costs with this model of expanding PACE are modest. Medicaid and PACE programs will need data to anchor negotiations to settle initial prices and packages of services. If the program aims for rapid expansion, personnel recruitment and training costs might be substantial. Contracting with existing and expanding businesses will require some time. PACE centers might need to be expanded or to have alternative sites contracted. Each of the initial sites will need to develop specific business plans.

Perhaps CMMI will fund these investments in their portfolio of models to test. However, if the site needs to raise the start-up costs, would it be helpful for investors to foot these costs, or for some level of government to offer a pay for success deal? At least in the first years of developing this model, it seems unwise to have investor interests competing with the interests of frail elders and their families for the funds made available by prudent medical care, as would happen in conventional for-profit business. However, a social impact bond could work because it would have a limited and agreed return on investment, perhaps with payment delayed to allow a well-developed start-up phase.

Pay for success does not have much of a track record in health care, but that approach would allow a governmental agency to enable a private business to take the risks that this will not work and, when it does work well, would pay a bonus sum for having taken that risk. This would seem to align with the useful incentives, but it may not really be necessary since there should be enough savings from more prudent medical care to limit the downside risks for a financially healthy PACE program.

7.7 After the first set of PACE expansion initiatives, how might MediCaring Communities develop?

The first set of communities should probably include about twelve to twenty communities. They should be connected by an improvement collaborative and technical assistance, both to accelerate their progress and to build tools and advisories to help the next set of communities. Some of these will be convincing successes within two years, and the insights from studying their progress should help shape the next cohort. Assuming that the trend is strongly favorable, the next cohort should be 50-75 communities starting about 2.5 years after the first cohort, and they should have the benefit of established pathways for clinical care, Community Board activation, savings calculation, expansion timing, and a dozen other elements of the work. A higher proportion of them will succeed convincingly within two years, and again there should be technical assistance and collaboration that builds the expertise to succeed more quickly and reliably. Depending upon the enthusiasm of communities and the results to date, a third cohort starting about 5 years after the first cohort would include perhaps 250-300 communities, and at this point, the demonstration would become a regular part of Medicare with conditions of participation and established quality reporting.

Assuming that the first cohort succeeds and attracts attention, during the second cohort, other kinds of health care providers will probably demand to expand the participating platforms. Some will want to establish new PACE programs that immediately expand PACE and rapidly take on the responsibilities of MediCaring Communities. Some will want to build MediCaring Communities on an ACO or MCO platform, which will require new waivers and demonstration authorities. Some communities that want and need a MediCaring approach will have many challenges to organizing any Community Board. Some may want to organize MediCaring Communities as a for-profit endeavor. Much of the evidence that will guide policy at that point is yet to be garnered in those first pilots. With the advantages of established methods and metrics, entirely new PACE programs can probably come up to speed quickly enough to allow them to be expansion population providers from the start. Adapting to ACO or MCO financing is easily done with a few critical waivers, if management and clinical leaders are committed to the clinical service reforms and the community can generate a strong Community Board. As MediCaring Communities become more widespread, policy will have to tackle the more challenging communities, and having technical assistance and collaboration would help achieve successes. The characteristics that make a community challenging for a MediCaring Community program are not those that usually make communities vulnerable, such as poverty or minority race and ethnic groups. Instead, MediCaring Communities are predicted to be more difficult in communities that have little tradition of joint action among coalitions, that have densely overlapping medical care and aging network providers, or that have very large or very small populations.

If for-profit management is to be allowed, the returns on investment probably need to follow a social impact bond structure, since having investor interests compete with the needs of elders and the interests to protect the Medicare Trust Fund and public financing generally would be destructive to public trust and potentially raise costs.

The first five components of MediCaring Communities would continue into the future: targeting frail elders in a geographic community, generating individual care plans for each, ensuring geriatric medical care, buttressing social and supportive services, and developing and adhering to the priorities of the community as to investments. However, the financing model will begin to become inadequate as the numbers of frail elders keeps increasing and the standards of MediCaring medical care become more widespread. Financing will come to rely upon a combination of social insurance and enhanced savings (as personal savings or as long-term care insurance), as outlined in Core Component #6 (page 103) so that the improved care system that MediCaring Communities develops is able to expand to serve a larger number of elders.

Chapter 8: Forging the Will

All these good ideas and evidence of potential improvements are without force unless the citizenry demands reforms and refuses to accept partial solutions that jeopardize achieving the full potential. Citizens facing frailty in old age, which is all of us who don't die while younger, have to become upset enough to raise our voices, demand improvement, enable political leaders to take on the issues, and insist upon learning how to make it all work, all across the country. This is a tall order, since we are still in a phase of inattention and failure to notice the shared experience of widespread suffering and frustration, along with inept services and inflated costs. Probably, family caregivers (present, past, and future) will need to rise up and demand attention to the plight of the frail elders they support and the family that is, was, or will be trying to cope. In addition, those responsible for public finance will be forced to take notice as the numbers rise and the costs escalate. But powerful forces are invested in the *status quo*, including simple familiarity and habit as well as financial interests and professional authority. Proving we can do better for our elders, our society, and ourselves, will be a triumph. The way to prove that is to launch pilot MediCaring Communities now, with resources we already have but can use more wisely. Showing it is possible is the answer to those who will say it can't be done. With a few proven successes, spreading the promise of reliable and efficient care to all will be less of a struggle.

This movement will require strong advocacy groups. Currently, multiple skilled and insightful advocacy groups have formed around eldercare issues: Consumer Voice, OWL, WISER, Justice in Aging, Alzheimers Association, Caring Across Generations, National Alliance for Caregiving, National Council on Aging, AARP, and Caregiver Action Network, to name a few. The issues are of broad concern and perhaps groups concerned about the well-being of children and public services generally would weigh in, since otherwise health care for elders will continue to consume larger shares of public funds, making other investments more difficult. Citizens probably need to have sustained organizations in order to carry the day. When motivated citizens with well-considered agendas activate advocacy organizations to develop convergent demands, then reform takes shape.

This chapter responds to the following questions:

8.1 How can Americans become more aware of the challenges of frailty in the last phase of life and become familiar with the connections to public policy and historic service delivery arrangements?

8.2 What organizations and interests are likely to support or oppose the endeavor and what strategies might forge a consensus to proceed?

8.1 How can Americans become more aware of the challenges of frailty in the last phase of life and become familiar with the connections to public policy and historic service delivery arrangements?

Family caregiving is or will soon be the most widely shared experience among Americans, even more common than raising children. Currently, family caregivers often do not recognize that they are in this role, whether they have slowly taken it up or were thrown into it unexpectedly from a crisis. In either case, crossing a threshold into the caregiver role often passed without explicit notice. And family members try to do the best they can for their disabled elder, usually without being identified as an important part of the care plan by physicians and without payment, and often even without thanks. Many frail elders are living with cognitive failure, and their ability to recall names or attend to social graces is gone or rapidly fading. Yet the overwhelming majority of care for frail elders is given for free by family and friends.[207]

Family caregivers provide the potential locus for forcing attention and reform. Those now profiting from the waste and inefficiency of elder care will not suddenly be seized with moral outrage and demand to risk being disadvantaged by a more balanced and thoughtful approach, whether the stakeholders are physicians, health plans, hospitals, assisted living centers, nursing homes, or other providers. Political leaders are scared of being drawn into a black hole of need with long-term care. When one looks about for where the fulcrum is to change the future, the answer comes back to family caregivers, if only they knew what a raw deal they are getting.

Houle and Eckstrom have written a wonderful and infuriating book about Houle's parents experiences as they aged.[208,209] The series of

---

[207] (Freedman and Spillman 2014)
[208] (Houle and Eckstrom 2015)
[209] (Lynn 2015)

avoidable calamities visited on this old couple and their family caregiver is just outrageous. Eckstrom, a geriatrician, writes a chapter after every maddening complication as to how you could avoid this for your parent. I'm glad they wrote this up, and I hope it helps a lot of people. But really! A book about how to protect your elder from the care system that is supposed to be helping! We don't write about how to be sure that the obstetrician catches the baby or that the cardiologist can read the EKG. Why does anyone have to write about how the physician serving the older person should know to check for pain!

Many others have written on their troubling experiences with aging parents or spouses, so many that it seems to be a growth industry. Perhaps the most widely known is Atul Gawande's book *Being Mortal*, which conveys the frustration and urgency of improving care for the last years of life.[210] What is missing from this library of stories and advice is a clear path forward and a call to collective action. That's what MediCaring Communities provides.

Knowing what to demand is difficult for elderly persons and their families, and the widespread lack of familiarity with long-term survival with multiple chronic conditions and progressive disability makes most family caregivers into explorers in unfamiliar territory. Perhaps we should start with demanding simple confidence in the care system. Can any provider promise anything of importance from onset of frailty through to the end of life? Can every provider promise to deliver what matters most for frail elders and their families, through to the end of life? Can they promise to relieve or prevent symptoms, to respect the patient and family priorities, to be stewards of the patient and family resources, or to help make every day just as good as it can be? Or, as is usually the case now, can they only promise to try to do a decent job in their little corner of specialization and to try hard not to notice or take responsibility for the overall experience required of the elder and his or her family?

---

[210] (Gawande 2014)

When you listen to people talking about the last few years of very old people in their families, you hear many stories of constant anxiety, many errors, unnecessary burdens and suffering, and substantial costs – and people seem to assume that these are just the unfortunate normal. Sometimes, you hear a story of a last few years that went really well, and the storyteller will almost always say something that indicates that he or she feels that they were lucky that things turned out this way. We should not have to be lucky to get reliable services, and we should not be complacent about being put through undue suffering from such a costly and highly dysfunctional system.

We need to tell stories, to get people familiar with the language, the experiences, and the evaluation of the merits of current care pathways. We need to draw political leaders into the conversation. They have family, too; and most who are over a certain age have at least second-hand experience. They just have never had the connections illuminated between public policy and the perpetuation of the dysfunctional care system. The fact that Medicare is suspicious of the need for home visits by physicians and wary of paying for them makes house calls unlikely. The substantial payments for procedures and imaging studies make them attractive to provide, even in marginally useful situations. The underpayment of thoughtful counseling and continuity makes those much less likely to be available. The list goes on and on, and the problem is not just payment incentives. The organizing of the health care system by provider type prevents real continuity, and Medicare regulations allow the illusion of patient choice to trump the value of developing close connections among a limited array of provider organizations to support continuity of care. The broad underfunding and undervaluing of community-based services, such as home-delivered meals and adapted housing, means that efficient and desirable care plans are often simply unavailable. In scores of ways, the current wasteful and dysfunctional care system is sustained by current policies, mostly at the state and federal levels.

We do need to get past the usual reluctance to acknowledge decline and death as part of the lifespan experience. Pretending that this phase is simply not there does not make it vanish; instead, that pretense prevents us from taking the steps that would make good eldercare reliable and affordable. Many people, even political leaders, fear that the problem is so overwhelming that we just can't deal with it.[211] This book shows that this is not true. If we buckled down and implemented MediCaring Communities, starting with pilot programs to expand PACE, and if we also began to structure savings and long-term care insurance so that people have the financing needed, we could build a sustainable and reliable care system frail elders need. So, readers of this book need to spread the conviction that useful and efficient reform is possible and could get underway today. Living as well as possible in a period of decline before dying is important to having a good life overall.

We probably need some people to demand even more than MediCaring Communities—demand social insurance to cover all long-term services and supports, demand not just adequate food but desirable food, demand not just adequate housing but preferred housing, and so on. With more aggressive demands as part of the context, the reasonableness of community-based management of a budgeted care system will more readily be seen as moderate and reasonable.

Many worry that the elderly will rob children and young adults of their opportunities. That concern misses the critical and tight emotional and economic connection of the elders and the young. The emotional connection is obvious, as elderly people so much want successive generations to thrive. The economic connection takes a deeper understanding of the interaction of savings and production.[212] Quite simply, the economic engine of the country has to be strong enough to support services paid from contemporaneous earnings and savings. If that engine is too weak to spin off excess earnings and to maintain the value of savings, then there will not be the revenues that elders will need. This recognition has taken root in some countries,

---

[211] (Lindland, et al. 2015)
[212] (National Research Council 2012)

where productivity of young adults is taken as a strong goal of the social order. That idea has not taken root in this country yet, as evidenced by the high rate of unemployment and incarceration of our young people. Once all parts of the society recognize the importance of the education and opportunities for young people to the well-being of the elderly, the perception of the risks of the older generation overreaching will diminish.

Of course, the issue of supporting frail elders will get the attention that the issues deserve as the numbers of frail elders rise sharply, less than twenty years from now. And many people will see the connections to policy. And if we have not implemented serious reforms for service delivery and financing, many people will see what a trap we have built for our futures and our economy. The important reform is to get that attention now; and that will require organizing family caregivers, telling strong stories, pushing political leaders to recognize the impact of their choices, and, perhaps most important right now, being willing to innovate and test out concepts that have a good chance of working and that will teach us how to move ahead. That's MediCaring Communities.

8.2 What organizations and interests are likely to support or oppose the endeavor and what strategies might forge a consensus to proceed?

For themselves and their families when they are frail, virtually everyone wants a MediCaring approach. It ensures reliability, respects preferences and priorities, and reduces costs. But acting as defenders of the status quo and its rewards, one would expect powerful forces to reject this reform – implementing MediCaring Communities stands to reduce the revenues now going to health care and allied businesses and to reduce their power in the society. Meal delivery might be found to be more important than ready availability of a low yield, high cost drug. That comparison does not happen now.

The rising numbers of frail elderly people provide a helpful response to those concerned about reducing utilization of medical services. If we generally keep the medical service capacity from growing along with the numbers, all current supply can stay very busy, while the per capita costs go down. This won't work in every instance, but it will overall, and that effect stands to mitigate the impact on medical service providers of prudent reductions of medical services per elderly person.

What organizations are likely to take up the cause? The consumer groups that try to represent the frail elders and their families have had very limited power. Some caregiver group will probably catch the rising tide and organize political pressure to get things right for the family caregiver. The paid caregivers are gradually finding their voice in unions and organizations advocating for fair wages and benefits. Physicians and other professionals who serve this population find professional satisfaction in improving care and in making it easier to serve these patients well, so some professional organizations will be allies. Perhaps the largest array of groups that might take up advocating for MediCaring Communities are the many publicly funded programs that are now being starved of funds by the steady growth of health care costs. We might find allies among those looking to improve transportation infrastructure, parks and recreation, schools and early childhood development, and all the other initiatives that are being crowded out by health care costs.[213]

The country has swung deeply into divisiveness and polarity and our political processes seem to have been frozen in unproductive debates. To find our way back to allowing thoughtful policy development, having (current, future, and past) family caregivers ready to vote on the basis of policies supporting a better deal for frail elders and their caregivers is a promising strategy. Getting many people upset over long wait lists for life's essentials, such as food, may well tap into both our fellow-feeling and our fears that we will be next to be in need without services to meet that need. Creating a climate of urgency that enables innovation and learning would help get MediCaring

---

[213] (Berwick, Report from Xanadu. Institute for Healthcare Improvement (IHI) 26th Annual National Forum Keynote Address 2014)

Communities onto the list of current policy issues. Many cities, counties, and states are interested. A push from Congress or a hot topic in visible political campaigns would break that open. This reform turns out to meld the best of the current political philosophies. It returns control to local communities and limits costs to government, it returns choices to elders and their families, and it takes responsibility for all frail elders in the community. Building MediCaring Communities is both compassionate conservatism and pragmatic social responsibility.

The cost of a pilot to expand PACE on a MediCaring Communities model is trivial, the risks to beneficiaries are very small, and the likely improvements are substantial. Indeed, the potential return is a sustainable and reliable care system.

So, do what you can. Push your Congressional representatives and state officials to allow MediCaring Communities to proceed and to get serious about encouraging savings and insurance for LTSS. Encourage consumer and professional organizations to join in. Get angry when your frail elders don't get good care. Encourage employers to focus on supporting family caregiving. If you have a PACE program in your community, see if their leadership is interested and help them plan. Write to your newspapers, call your radio and TV outlets, and tell them about a way forward with MediCaring Communities and PACE expansion. Subscribe to the email newsletter at MediCaring.org, where up to date information and activist suggestions will be posted. Tell us about improvements you see to this book and its plans by sending an email message to *info@medicaring.org*. Help to build a citizen and caregiver voice in public policy! We can do this.

A Final Word

On an ill-advised rafting trip several years ago, I was bruised and battered after tumbling into the raging waters. I found myself scrambling onto a rock in the middle of the river—my raft and mates ahead, all of us trying to hold steady. The last thing I wanted to do was to jump back in. My initial relief about the safety of my rock was doomed to be temporary. I had to plunge into the dangerous current and swim, hoping for the best.

That's how most people feel about navigating the increasingly difficult currents of living to be very old in America. We cling to a fragile and temporary security created by personal savings and family, and public programs like Medicare, Medicaid, the Older Americans Act, which, along with charitable social services, have kept so many afloat in the past. But the situation is becoming much more hazardous—one full of dangerous and deadly undercurrents of rapidly increasing numbers of frail elders with thin savings and poorly funded supportive services, medical overtreatment, and multiplying health care costs. We need to confront the inevitability of change.

We simply cannot keep the future working like the past. If some of us insist on clinging to that rock, hoping for a miraculous rescue from an unknown source, millions of our fellow travelers will experience devastating consequences, as services become unavailable while suffering and costs explode. The political power of the elderly might then shred the fabric of society, as essential investments in healthy children and a healthy economy become impossible.

Even worse, if we fail to tackle the challenges of right-sizing services for a much larger population of very old people, we are likely to be forced to choose who to pull from the river, and who to leave behind. We could attempt to sustain the illusion of helping by providing the existing supports and services to an ever-shrinking proportion of those in need, while learning to accept that others will not have adequate housing, food, and health care, or simply finding ways to be blind to their plight.

That path is unacceptable. Who among us wants to be saved from suffering and destitution while our friends and loved ones are not? Who wants to risk being among those abandoned? Tradition and culture guarantee that we are all in this together. We will have to take our chances, jump in, and swim to an uncertain future. Planning ahead, testing the options, and putting better arrangements in place now will make us much more likely to succeed, and building MediCaring Communities through PACE expansion is a comprehensive, practical model that can get us started toward a much better place.

We did not, of course, plan for this journey with the idea that we would wind up stuck on a rock in an increasingly threatening environment. Decades ago, we funded a health care system that was well-suited to the needs and realities of those times. But circumstances have changed, and our systems must now change, too.

The essential first step is to understand our new set of facts and to develop a new set of insights. This book has shown that we can build our future in a way that treats us all fairly as we age, and achieves reliability and efficiency. Success is possible. We can get through the next fifty years of a rapidly aging society, having cared well for one another, and having avoided slowing our overall economic development. We do need, though, to be honest about the facts and willing to work with reality.

The journey will entail some risks, and failing to get underway will only make it harder to succeed. When I plunged into the rapids, I had some strengths to build on. I could swim; I wore a helmet; and my comrades were ready to try to help. So too, our society will improve our chances of building the care system that delivers what we most need in frail old age if we build on our strengths, marshall our resources, deliberately plan for what's ahead, and encourage and support one another along the way. We may occasionally wash up in a spot that turns out to be disappointing, but we will learn from that, and move on.

Doing nothing, we can continue to hang onto our metaphorical rock a while longer. But eventually, even that hard work will fail and many of us will face grim futures of disability without essential services.

We have a long national tradition of joining forces to solve seemingly intractable problems and challenges. We can encourage innovation, learn from experience, abandon outmoded practices, and embrace a worthy future. The time has come to jump in and solve the problems, and this book charts the course.

Glossary

AAA – Area Agency on Aging. An agency (in a local government or a community-based organization) that provides information on resources in the local area. An AAA is available in every part of the country, funded by the Older Americans Act.

ACL – Administration for Community Living. An agency that is part of the Department of Health and Human Services and manages programs to serve persons in old age and those with disabilities.

ADL – Activities of Daily Living. A term used in healthcare to refer to people's daily self-care activities.

ADRC – Aging and Disability Resource Center. An agency that provides a consolidated source of information about aging, disability, and the services in the local area.

ACO – Accountable Care Organization. An organization of health care providers that continue to be paid fee-for-service; but, if they can achieve savings (compared with usual care), they share the savings with Medicare and other insurers. CMS has established a few types of ACOs, including Pioneer, Next Generation, and Medicare Shared Savings Plans.

AHRQ – Agency for Healthcare Research and Quality. The federal agency that sponsors health services research.

AoA – Administration on Aging. A Federal agency now incorporated into the Administration for Community Living that focuses on community-based supports and protections for elders.

BPCI – Bundled Payment Care Improvement Program in Medicare, which provides incentives for hospital and post-hospital core efficiencies.

CARE – The Continuity Assessment Record and Evaluation. A group of geriatric patient assessment tools with standardized items that was intended for use across settings where patients receive care and which did serve as the source for much of the latest version of OASIS and MDS.

Caregiver – A person who is providing direct services, supervision, or coordination of services on behalf of a frail elderly person.

CCM – Chronic Care Management code. A new billing code in 2016 for which Medicare pays for ongoing management of health care by a physician practice for persons living with chronic conditions.

CMMI – Center for Medicare and Medicaid Innovation. The part of CMS that administers innovative projects to improve system performance.

CMS – Centers for Medicare & Medicaid Services (*cms.gov*). The federal agency that administers Medicare and Medicaid programs.

Community Board – The collected group of stakeholders that generate a community's voice to decide evidence-informed priorities for improving elder care in a MediCaring Community.

CQI – Continuous quality improvement. A set of management tools to guide identifying, testing, and learning from innovations.

CRISP – Chesapeake Regional Information System, or CRISP (*crisphealth.org*), is a regional health information exchange (HIE) serving Maryland and the District of Columbia.

ED or ER – Emergency Department or Emergency Room. A part of a hospital for receiving newly sick or injured persons.

Frail elders (or frail elderly people, or just "elders") are people living with disabilities and illnesses that are generally associated with aging and that tend to worsen through to death. Operationally, this category might be defined as having ADL dependencies or poor judgement requiring assistance or supervision by others for most of each day, or having conditions or age likely to come to this point in the near future. Frailty is mainly a lack of reserve so that challenges to health or living circumstances have more severe results than they would in a younger person with more resiliency. See also *Component #1: Frail Elders Identified in a Geographic Community* (page 7).

Family – In this writing, we use "family" to include all those who are bonded to a particular elder by affection, legal relationship, or other operation of the law. The category includes diverse kinds of relationships, so long as the well-being of the frail elderly person is a personal concern.

GRACE – Geriatric Resources for Assessment and Care of Elders. A model of service delivery especially focused on low-income seniors.

HCBS – Home and Community-Based Services. Both a general approach to supporting frail and disabled persons at home rather than in an institution and a specific program such as the one in the Veterans Health System in which an IDT serves persons with advanced illnesses and disabilities at home. See also *Component #3: Medical Care Tailored to Frail Elders* (page 47).

HIE – Health Information Exchange. A regional health care information network implementing connections, data standards, and data management that enable interoperability and interchange of information across health care providers, usually on a regional basis.

HIPAA – Health Insurance Portability and Accountability Act. The statute that, among other things, standardizes the privacy rules for medical records.

IAH – Independence at Home. A Congressionally mandated demonstration program of in-home care by physicians with a geriatric focus. See also Chapter 3

IDT – interdisciplinary team. The team that together provides care planning and service delivery for a frail elderly person. An IDT always includes a physician (or nurse practitioner), nurse, and a person from a social work or psychology background and might also include many other specialists and personal care workers.

IOM – Institute of Medicine, now National Academy of Medicine. Part of the National Academy of Sciences, and often the lead in putting together influential statements of the scientific evidence around policy issues.

IMPACT – Improving Medicare Post-Acute Care Transformation, a federal statute that requires that provider organizations that serve Medicare patients after hospitalization will provide assessments in a required uniform way, to enable comparisons of outcomes with different strategies for services.

LTSS – Long-Term Services and Supports. Basically, all the non-medical elements that go into supporting a frail elder across time, such as assistance with bathing and dressing.

MCO – Managed Care Organization. An organization that receives a monthly capitation (PMPM) and is obligated to provide all covered services that the enrolled population needs.

MDS – Minimum Data Set. The Minimum Data Set (MDS) is part of the U.S. federally mandated process for clinical assessment of all residents in Medicare or Medicaid certified nursing homes.

OASIS – Outcome and Assessment Information Set is the Medicare-mandated standard clinical assessment tool for persons receiving home care.

PACE – Program of All-Inclusive Care for the Elderly. A permanent delivery system and payment arrangement that serves persons living in the community and needing a nursing home level of care. PACE now mostly serves persons who are eligible for both Medicare and Medicaid coverage. See also *Chapter 7: Implementation: Start with PACE* (page 123).

PCP – Primary Care Provider. The physician who takes responsibility for the range of health care needs of a patient, including prevention, rehabilitation, and outpatient diagnosis and treatment. Usually, this category is operationalized as internal medicine, family practice, general practice, pediatrics and geriatrics, though specialist physicians can take on this role as well.

PCORI – Patient-Centered Outcomes Research Institute. Federally chartered funder of research to guide patient and provider decisions with evidence.

Physician – The medical care provider with skills and license to take responsibility for health care of patients, a category which includes nurse practitioners and, in some situations, physician assistants.

PMPM – Per member per month. The amount paid by an insurer (e.g., Medicare or Medicaid) to a capitated provider, or the cost of services when allocated evenly across the relevant patient population.

ROI – A performance measure used to evaluate the efficiency of an investment or to compare the efficiency of a number of different investments. ROI measures the amount of return on an investment relative to the investment's cost. To calculate ROI, the benefit (or return) of an investment is divided by the cost of the investment, and the result is expressed as a percentage or a ratio.

Bibliography

Administration on Aging, Administration for Community Living, A Profile of Older Americans. 2014. Accessed February 15, 2016. http://www.aoa.acl.gov/-aging_statistics/profile/index.aspx.

Administration on Aging, Administration for Community Living, Eldercare Locator. n.d. Accessed October 19, 2015. http://www.eldercare.gov/Eldercare.NET/-Public/Index.aspx.

Administration on Aging, Administration for Community Living, Projected Future Growth of the Older Population. 2005. Accessed October 22, 2015. http://www.aoa.acl.gov/aging_statistics/future_growth/future_growth.aspx#aging.

Agency for Healthcare Research and Quality. 2013. "System-Integrated Program Coordinates Care for People With Advanced Illness, Leading to Greater Use of Hospice Services, Lower Utilization and Costs, and High Satisfaction." October 23. Accessed March 4, 2016. https://innovations.ahrq.gov/profiles/system-integrated-program-coordinates-care-people-advanced-illness-leading-greater-use.

Agency for Healthcare Research and Quality, TeamSTEPPS®: Strategies and Tools to Enhance Performance and Patient Safety. n.d. Accessed October 19, 2015. http://www.ahrq.gov/professionals/education/curriculum-tools/teamstepps/index.html.

Ahalt, C, L C Walter, L Yourman, C Eng, E J Perez-Stable, and A K Smith. 2012. ""Knowing is better": preferences of diverse older adults for discussing prognosis." *Journal of the American Geriatrics Society* 27 (5): 568-75.

American Geriatrics Society Choosing Wisely Workgroup. 2013. "American Geriatrics Society Identifies Five Things That Healthcare Providers and Patients Should Question." Accessed February 29, 2016. http://www.choosingwisely.org/societies/american-geriatrics-society/.

American Geriatrics Society Expert Panel on Person-Centered Care. 2015. "Person-Centered Care: A Definition and Essential Elements." *Journal of the American Geriatrics Society.* doi:10.1111/jgs.13866.

American Geriatrics Society Expert Panel on the Care of Older Adults. 2012. "Guiding Principles for the Care of Older Adults with Multimorbidity: An Approach for Clinicians." *Journal of the American Geriatrics Society* 60 (10): E1-E25.

Beales, J L, and T Edes. 2009. "Veteran's Affairs Home-Based Primary Care." *Clinics in Geriatric Medicine* 25 (1): 149-54.

Beauchamp, J, V Cheh, R Schmitz, P Kemper, and J Hall. 2008. *The Effect of the Program of All-Inclusive Care for the Elderly on Quality.* Mathematica Policy Research, Inc. Accessed March 2, 2016. https://www.cms.gov/Research-Statistics-Data-and-Systems/Statistics-Trends-and-Reports/Reports/downloads/beauchamp_2008.pdf.

Berenson, R, and E Docteur. 2013. "Doing Better by Doing Less: Approaches to Tackle Overuse of Services." The Urban Institute . Accessed March 2, 2016. http://www.urban.org/research/publication/doing-better-doing-less-approaches-tackle-overuse-services.

Bernhardt, A, J Lynn, G Berger, J Lee, K Reuter, J DaVanzo, and A Dobson. 2016. "Making It Safe to Grow Old: A Financial Simulation Model for Launching MediCaring Communities for Frail Elderly Medicare Beneficiaries [published online ahead of print June 2016]." *Milbank Quarterly*.

Bernstein, N. 2014. "Fighting to Honor a Father's Last Wish: To Die at Home." September 25. Accessed March 3, 2016. http://www.nytimes.com/-2014/09/26/nyregion/family-fights-health-care-system-for-simple-request-to-die-at-home.html?_r=0.

Berwick, D M. 2014. "Report from Xanadu. Institute for Healthcare Improvement (IHI) 26th Annual National Forum Keynote Address." December. Accessed February 18, 2016. https://www.youtube.com/watch?v=qG8Fcr4tAH8.

Berwick, D M, and A D Hackbarth. 2012. "Eliminating Waste in U.S. Health Care." *Journal of the American Medical Association* 307 (14): 1513-1516.

Bhaumik, U, K Norris, G Charron, S P Walker, S J Sommer , E Chan , D U Dickerson, S Nethersole, and E R Woods. 2013. "A cost analysis for a community-based case management intervention program for pediatric asthma." *J Asthma* 50 (3): 310-7.

Bischoff, K E, R Sudore, Y Miao, W J Boscardin, and A K Smith. 2013. "Advance Care Planning and the Quality of End-of-Life Care in Older Adults." *Journal of the American Geriatrics Society* 61 (2): 209-214.

Bokhour, B G. 2006. "Communication in interdisciplinary team meetings: What are we talking about?" *Journal of Interprofessional Care* 20 (4): 349-363.

Boult, C, B Leff, C M Boyd, J L Wolff, J A Marsteller, K D Frick, S Wegener, et al. 2013. "A Matched-Pair Cluster-Randomized Trial of Guided Care for High-Risk Older Patients." *Journal of General Internal Medicine* 28 (5): 612-21.

Boutwell, A E, M B Johnson, and R Watkins. in press . "An Analysis of a Social Work-based Model of Transitional Care to Reduce Hospital Readmissions: Preliminary Data." *Journal of the American Geriatrics Society*.

Bradley, E, and L Taylor. 2013. *The American Health Care Paradox: Why Spending More is Getting Us Less*. New York, NY: Public Affairs.

Brown, R S, D Peikes, G Peterson, J Schore, and C M Razafindrakoto. 2012. "Six Features of Medicare Coordinated Care Demonstration Programs that Cut Hospital Admissions of High-Risk Patients." *Health Affairs* 31 (6): 1156-1166.

Buchbinder, R, R H Osborne, P R Ebeling, J D Wark, P Mitchell, C Wriedt, S Graves, M P Staples, and B Murphy. 2009. "A Randomized Trial of Vertebroplasty for Painful Osteoporotic Vertebral Fractures." *New England Journal of Medicine* 361 (6): 557-568.

Burwell, S M. 2015. "Setting Value-Based Payment Goals — HHS Efforts to Improve U.S. Health Care." *New England Journal of Medicine* 372 (10): 897-899.

Care Transitions Intervention. n.d. *About the Care Transitions Intervention.* Accessed February 11, 2016. http://caretransitions.org/about-the-care-transitions-intervention/.

Caregiver Corps Act of 2014, S.2842. 2014. September 17. Accessed February 17, 2016. https://www.congress.gov/bill/113th-congress/senate-bill/2842.

Cassel, C K, and J A Guest. 2012. "Choosing Wisely: Helping Physicians and Patients Make Smart Decisions About Their Care." *Journal of the American Medical Association* 307 (17): 1801-1802.

Caverly, T J, A Fagerlin, B Zikmund-Fisher, S Kirsh, J T Kullgren, K Prenovost, and E A Kerr. 2015. "Appropriate Prescribing for Patients With Diabetes at High Risk for Hypoglycemia: National Survey of Veterans Affairs Health Care Professionals ." *JAMA Internal Medicine.* http://archinte.jamanetwork.com/article.aspx?articleid=2466631.

Centers for Medicare and Medicaid Services Measures Inventory. 2016. February 14. Accessed February 19, 2016. https://www.cms.gov/Medicare/Quality-Initiatives-Patient-Assessment-Instruments/QualityMeasures/CMS-Measures-Inventory.html.

Centers for Medicare and Medicaid Services, 80 FR 42168. 2015. "Medicare and Medicaid Programs; Reform of Requirements for Long-Term Care Facilities." July 16. Accessed February 17, 2016. https://www.federalregister.gov/articles/2015/07/16/2015-17207/medicare-and-medicaid-programs-reform-of-requirements-for-long-term-care-facilities.

Centers for Medicare and Medicaid Services, Affordable Care Act payment model saves more than $25 million in first performance year. 2015. Accessed January 19, 2016. https://www.cms.gov/Newsroom/MediaReleaseDatabase/Press-releases/2015-Press-releases-items/2015-06-18.html.

Centers for Medicare and Medicaid Services, Balancing Incentives Program. n.d. Accessed March 9, 2016. https://www.medicaid.gov/Medicaid-CHIP-Program-Information/By-Topics/Long-Term-Services-and-Supports/Balancing/Balancing-Incentive-Program.html.

Centers for Medicare and Medicaid Services, CARE Item Set and B-CARE. 2015. January 13. Accessed February 16, 2016. https://www.cms.gov/Medicare/-Quality-Initiatives-Patient-Assessment-Instruments/Post-Acute-Care-Quality-Initiatives/CARE-Item-Set-and-B-CARE.html.

Centers for Medicare and Medicaid Services, Chronic Care Management Regulation, 79 FR 67715. 2014. "Medicare Program; Revisions to Payment Policies Under the Physician Fee Schedule." November 13. Accessed February 17, 2016. https://www.cms.gov/Medicare/Medicare-Fee-for-Service-

Payment/PhysicianFeeSched/PFS-Federal-Regulation-Notices-Items/CMS-1612-FC.html.

Centers for Medicare and Medicaid Services, Chronic Conditions Among Medicare Beneficiaries. 2012. Accessed February 11, 2016. https://www.cms.gov/-Research-Statistics-Data-and-Systems/Statistics-Trends-and-Reports/Chronic-Conditions/Chartbook_Charts.html.

Centers for Medicare and Medicaid Services, Independence at Home (IAH) Demonstration: Year 1 Practice Results. 2015. Accessed January 19, 2016. http://innovation.cms.gov/initiatives/Independence-at-Home/.

Centers for Medicare and Medicaid Services, MDS 3.0 RAI Manual. 2016. January 28. Accessed February 16, 2016. https://www.cms.gov/Medicare/Quality-Initiatives-Patient-Assessment-Instruments/NursinghomeQualityInits/-MDS30RAIManual.html.

Centers for Medicare and Medicaid Services, Money Follows the Person. n.d. Accessed March 9, 2016. https://www.medicaid.gov/medicaid-chip-program-information/by-topics/long-term-services-and-supports/balancing/money-follows-the-person.html.

Centers for Medicare and Medicaid Services, Outcome and Assessment Information Set (OASIS). 2012. April 5. Accessed February 16, 2016. https://www.cms.gov/Medicare/Quality-Initiatives-Patient-Assessment-Instruments/OASIS/index.html?redirect=/oasis/01_overview.asp.

Centers for Medicare and Medicaid Services, Regulations and Guidance Manuals. Programs of All-Inclusive Care for the Elderly (PACE) Rev. 2. 2011. Accessed February 15, 2016. https://www.cms.gov/Regulations-and-Guidance/-Guidance/Manuals/downloads/pace111c08.pdf.

Choosing Wisely. 2016. *Choosing Wisely: An Initiative of the ABIM Foundation.* Accessed February 12, 2016. http://www.choosingwisely.org/.

Ciemens, E L, B Stuart, R Gerber, J Newman, and M Bauman. 2006. "An Evaluation of the Advanced Illness Management (AIM) Program: Increasing Hospice Utilization in the San Francisco Bay Area." *Journal of Palliative Medicine* 9 (6): 1401-1411.

Coleman, E A, C Parry, S Chalmers, and SJ Min. 2006. "The Care Transitions Intervention: Results of a Randomized Controlled Trial." *Archives of Internal Medicine* 166: 1822-1828.

Counsell, S R, C M Callahan, W Tu, T E Stump, and G W Arling. 2009. "Cost Analysis of the Geriatric Resources for Assessment and Care of Elders Care Management Intervention." *Journal of the American Geriatrics Society* 57 (8): 1420-1426.

Deming, W E. 1994. *The New Economics for Industry, Government, Education.* Cambridge, MA: Massachusetts Institute of Technology .

Department of Labor. n.d. "We Count on Home Care: U.S. Court of Appeals Unanimously Upheld DOL Rule, Opinion Effective as of Oct. 13, 2015." Accessed March 9, 2016. http://www.dol.gov/whd/homecare/litigation.htm.

Dobson, A, L DaVanzo, A M El-Gamil, S Heath, M Shimer, G Berger, A Pick, N Manolav, and J M Freeman. 2012. "Clinically Appropriate and Cost-Effective Placement: Improving Health Care Quality and Effiiciency." Dobson DaVanzo. Accessed March 2, 2016. http://www.ahhqi.org/images/pdf/cacep-report.pdf.

Edes, T, B Kinosian, N H Vuckovic, L O Nichols, M M Becker, and M Hossain. 2014. "Better Access, Quality, and Cost for Clinically Complex Veterans with Home-Based Primary Care." *Journal of the American Geriatrics Society* 62 (10): 1954-1961.

Eiken, S, K Sredl, B Burwell, and P Saucier. 2015. "Medicaid Expenditures for Long-Term Services and Supports (LTSS) in FY 2013: Home and Community-Based Services Were a Majority of LTSS Spending." Truven Health Analytics. Accessed November 18, 2015. http://www.medicaid.gov/medicaid-chip-program-information/by-topics/long-term-services-and-supports/long-term-services-and-supports.html.

Favreault, M M, H Gleckman, and R Johnson. 2015. "Financing Long-Term Services And Supports: Options Reflect Trade-Offs For Older Americans And Federal Spending." *Health Affairs* 34 (12): 2181-91.

Favreault, M, and J Dey. 2015. "Long-Term Services and Supports for Older Americans: Risks and Financing Research Brief." Urban Institute and Milliman. Accessed March 28, 2016. http://aspe.hhs.gov/basic-report/long-term-services-and-supports-older-americans-risks-and-financing-research-brief.

Freedman, V A, and B C Spillman. 2014. "Disability and Care Needs Among Older Americans." *Milbank Quarterly* 92 (3): 509-541.

Fried, L P, C M Tangen, J Walston, A B Newman, C Hirsch, J Gottdiener, T Seeman, et al. 2001. "Frailty in Older Adults: Evidence for a Phenotype." *The Journals of Gerontology. Series A, Biological Sciences and Medical Sciences* 56 (3): M146-156.

Garber, L and the S & I Framework. 2014. "The Plan of Care (Conditions, Goals and Interventions), along with Risk Factors and Decision Modifiers, iteratively evolve over time. Adapted from the work of Lawrence Garber, MD, with the S&I Framework.Slide 42." September 19. Accessed April 20, 2016. http://wiki.siframework.org/file/view/LCC%20Closing%20Ceremony%2028S EP14_for_delivery.pptx/525009000/LCC%20Closing%20Ceremony%2028SE P14_for_delivery.pptx.

Gardner, R C, V Valcour, and K Yaffe. 2013. "Dementia in the oldest old: a multi-factorial and growing public health issue." *Alzheimers Research and Therapy* 5 (4): 27.

Gawande, A. 2014. *Being Mortal: Medicine and What Matters in the End.* New York, NY: Metropolitan Books, Henry Holt and Company, LLC.

Ghosh, A, C Orfield, and R Schmitz. 2014. "Evaluating PACE: A Review of the Literature." Accessed March 28, 2016. https://aspe.hhs.gov/basic-report/-evaluating-pace-review-literature.

Government Offices of Sweden. n.d. *Municipalities and county councils.* Accessed February 12, 2016. http://www.government.se/government-policy/-municipalities-and-county-councils/.

Harrell, R, J Lynott, S Guzman, and C Lampkin. 2014. "What Is Livable? Community Preferences of Older Adults." Accessed April 4, 2016. http://www.aarp.org/-ppi/issues/livable-communities/info-2015/what-is-livable-AARP-ppi-liv-com.html.

Hartford Institute for Geriatric Nursing. 2016. "Hartford Institute for Geriatric Nursing, Geriatric Interdisciplinary Team Training(GITT)." Accessed February 29, 2016. http://hartfordign.org/practice/gitt/.

Hayes, K, G W Hoagland, N Lopez, L Rosner, B Collins, M Workman, and K Taylor. 2016. "Initial Recommendations to Improve the Financing of Long-Term Care." Bipartisan Policy Center. Accessed February 17, 2016. http://bipartisanpolicy.org/library/long-term-care-financing-recommendations/.

Health and Retirement Study. 2016. Accessed February 29, 2016. http://hrsonline.isr.umich.edu/.

Health Insurance Portability and Accountability Act of 1996, P.L. 104-191. 1996. August 21. Accessed February 17, 2016. https://www.cms.gov/Regulations-and-Guidance/HIPAA-Administrative-Simplification/HIPAAGenInfo/-downloads/hipaalaw.pdf.

Himmelstein, D U, D Thorne, E Warren, and S Woolhandler. 2009. "Medical Bankruptcy in the United States, 2007: Results of a National Study." *American Journal of Medicine* 122 (8): 741-746.

HITECH Answers. n.d. "HITECH Act Summary." Accessed March 9, 2016. http://www.hitechanswers.net/about/about-the-hitech-act-of-2009/.

Hogan, B E, W Linden, and B Najarian. 2002. "Social support interventions: Do they work?" *Clinical Psychology Review* 22 (3): 381-442.

Holland, S K, S R Evered, and B A Center. 2014. "Long-term care benefits may reduce end-of-life medical care costs." *Population Health Management* 17 (6): 332-339.

Holmes, Oliver Wendell. 2009. *The One-Hoss Shay, How the Old Horse Won the Bet, & the Broomstick Train.* Bennington, NH: Flying Chipmunk Publishing.

Hong, C S, A L Siegel, and T G Ferris. 2014. "Caring for High-Need, High-Cost Patients: What Makes for a Successful Care Management Program?"

Commonwealth Fund. Accessed January 19, 2016. http://www.commonwealthfund.org/publications/issue-briefs/2014/aug/-high-need-high-cost-patients.

Houle, M C, and E Eckstrom. 2015. *The Gift of Caring: Saving our Parents from the Perils of Modern Health Care*. Lanham, MD: Taylor Trade Publishing.

Improving Medicare Post-Acute Transformation Act of 2014, Public Law 113-185. 2014. October 6. Accessed February 16, 2016. https://www.congress.gov/-bill/113th-congress/house-bill/4994/text/pl.

Institute of Medicine. 2014. "Dying in America: Improving Quality and Honoring Individual Preferences Near the End of Life." National Academies Press. Accessed January 19, 2016. http://iom.nationalacademies.org/Reports/-2014/Dying-In-America-Improving-Quality-and-Honoring-Individual-Preferences-Near-the-End-of-Life.aspx.

Jack, B W, V K Chetty, D Anthony, J L Greenwald, G M Sanchez, A E Johnson, S R Forsythe, et al. 2009. "A Reengineered Hospital Discharge Program to Decrease Rehospitalization: A Randomized Trial." *Annals of Internal Medicine* 150 (3): 178-188.

Jayadevappa, R S, S Chhatre, M Weiner, and D B Raziano. 2006. "Health Resource Utilization and Medical Care Cost of Acute Care Elderly Unit Patients." *Value in Health* 9 (3): 186-192.

JEN Associates. 2013. "Massachusetts PACE Evaluation: Nursing Facility Residency and Mortality." November 23. Accessed April 14, 2016. http://www.mass.gov/eohhs/docs/masshealth/pace/ma-pace-evaluation-nf-residency-and-mortality-summary-report-11-23-15.pdf.

Kallmes, D F, B A Comstock, P J Heagerty, J A Turner, D J Wilson, T H Diamond, R Edwards, et al. 2009. "A Randomized Trial of Vertebroplasty for Osteoporotic Spinal Fractures." *New England Journal of Medicine* 361 (6): 569-579.

Kane, R L, P Homyak, B Bershadsky, and S Flood. 2006. "The Effects of a Variant of the Program for All-Inclusive Care for the Elderly on Hospital and Utilization and Outcomes." *The Journal of the American Geriatrics Society* 54 (2): 276-283.

Karnick, P, H Margellos-Anast, G Seals, S Whitman, G Aljadeff, and D Johnson. 2007. "The pediatric asthma intervention: a comprehensive cost-effective approach to asthma management in a disadvantaged inner-city community." *J Asthma* 44 (1): 39-44. doi:doi: 10.1080/0277090060112539.

Keenan, T A. 2010. "Home and Community Preferences of the 45+ Population." AARP. Accessed January 19, 2016. http://www.aarp.org/research/topics/-community/info-2014/home-community-services-10.html.

Krakauer, R, C M Spettell, L Reisman, and M J Wade. 2009. "Opportunities to Improve the Quality of Care for Advanced Illness: An Aetna Pilot Program shows how it can be done." *Health Affairs* 28 (5): 1357-1359.

LeadingAge. 2016. "LeadingAge Pathways Report: Perspectives on the Challenges of Financing Long-Term Services and Supports." February. Accessed March 4, 2016. https://www.leadingage.org/pathways/.

Lee, S J, W J Boscardin, I Stijacic-Cenzer, J Conell-Price, S O'Brien, and L C Walter. 2013. "Time lag to benefit after screening for breast and colorectal cancer: meta-analysis of survival data from the United States, Sweden, United Kingdom, and Denmark." *BMJ* 346 (e8441).

Lee, S, A Smith, E Widera, L Yourman, M Schonberg, and C Ahalt. n.d. *ePrognosis: Estimating Prognosis for Elders.* Accessed October 19, 2015. http://eprognosis.ucsf.edu.

Leff, B, L Burton, S L Mader, B Naughton, J Burl, S K Inouye, W B Greenough, et al. 2005. "Hospital to Home: Feasibility and Outcomes of a Program to Provide Hospital-level Care at Home for Acutely Ill Older Patients." *Annals of Internal Medicine* 143 (11): 798-808.

Leff, B, L Reider, K D Frick, D O Scharfstein, C M Boyd, K Frey, L Karm, and C Boult. 2009. "Guided Care and the Cost of Complex Healthcare: A Preliminary Report." *American Journal of Managed Care* 15 (8): 555-9.

Lindland, E, M Fond, A Haydon, and N Kendall-Taylor. 2015. "Gauging Aging: Mapping the Gaps between Expert and Public Understandings of Aging in America." The Frameworks Institute. Accessed December 7, 2015. http://www.frameworksinstitute.org/pubs/mtg/gaugingaging/index.html.

Linehan, K, and S Coberly. 2015. "Medicare's Post-Acute Care Payment:An Updated Review of the Issues and Policy Proposals." National Health Policy Forum. Accessed January 19, 2016. http://www.nhpf.org/library/details.cfm/2913.

Lynn, J. 2015. "Don't Accept Medical Errors as the Standard of Care for Frail Elders." *Medicaring.org.* September 28. Accessed October 19, 2015. http://medicaring.org/2015/09/28/dont-accept-medical-errors-as-the-standard-of-care/.

Lynn, J, and A Montgomery. 2015. "Creating a Comprehensive Care System for Frail Elders in "Age Boom" America." *The Gerontologist* 55 (2): 278-285.

Lynn, J, and E Blair. 2016. *Long-Term Care Is Back in Policy Debates!* March 28. Accessed April 4, 2016. http://medicaring.org/2016/03/28/long-term-care-is-back-in-policy-debates/.

Marquand, A. 2015. "Too Sick to Care: Direct Care Workers, Medicaid Expansion and the Coverage Gap." PHI National. Accessed January 19, 2016. http://phinational.org/policy/issues/health-coverage/too-sick-care-direct-care-workers-medicaid-expansion-and-coverage-gap.

Medicare Prescription Drug, Improvement, and Modernization Act, P.L. 108-173. 2003. December 8. Accessed March 4, 2016. https://www.gpo.gov/fdsys/-pkg/PLAW-108publ173/pdf/PLAW-108publ173.pdf.

MedPAC and MACPAC. 2015. "Beneficiaries Dually Eligible for Medicare and Medicaid." Accessed February 15, 2016. http://www.medpac.gov/-documents/data-book/january-2015-medpac-and-macpac-data-book-beneficiaries-dually-eligible-for-medicare-and-medicaid.pdf.

Mehdizadeh, S A, I M Nelson, and R A Applebaum. 2006. "Nursing Home Use in Ohio: Who Stays, Who Pays?" Scripps Gerontology Center at University of Miami. Accessed January 19, 2016. http://miamioh.edu/cas/-academics/centers/scripps/research/publications/2006/02/Nursing-Home-Use-Ohio-Who-Stays-Who-Pays_Brief_2006.html.

Meret-Hanke, L. 2011. "Effects of the Program of All-Inclusive Care for the Elderly on Hospital Use." *The Gerontologist* 51 (6): 774-785.

MetLife Mature Market Institute. 2011. "The MetLife Study of Caregiving Costs to Working Caregivers: Double Jeopardy for Baby Boomers Caring for Their Parents." Accessed November 13, 2015. https://www.metlife.com/-mmi/research/caregiving-cost-working-caregivers.html#key findings.

Meyer, H. 2011. "A new care paradigm slashes hospital use and nursing home stays for the elderly and the physically and mentally disabled." *Health Affairs* 30 (3): 412-415.

Minnesota Department of Human Services. 2016. *MnCHOICES*. January 21. Accessed February 16, 2016. http://www.dhs.state.mn.us/main/-idcplg?IdcService=GET_DYNAMIC_CONVERSION&RevisionSelectionMet hod=LatestReleased&dDocName=dhs16_180264.

Mittelman, M S, W E Haley, O J Clay, and D L Roth. 2006. "Improving caregiver well-being delays nursing home placement of patients with Alzheimer's disease." *Neurology* 67 (9): 1592-1599.

Montgomery, A, and J Lynn. 2014. "The MediCaring Model: Best Plan for Frail Elders in the Longevity Era." *Public Policy and Aging Report* 24 (3): 112-117.

Murphy, D J, D Burrows, S Santilli, A W Kemp, S Tenner, B Kreling, and J Teno. 1994. "The Influence of the Probability of Survival on Patients' Preferences Regarding Cardiopulmonary Resuscitation." *New England Journal of Medicine* 330 (8): 545-549.

Musumeci, M. 2015. "Financial and Administrative Alignment Demonstrations for Dual Eligible Beneficiaries Compared: States with Memoranda of Understanding Approved by CMS." Kaiser Family Foundation. Accessed January 19, 2016. http://kff.org/medicaid/issue-brief/financial-alignment-demonstrations-for-dual-eligible-beneficiaries-compared/.

National Association of Area Agencies on Aging and Scripps Gerontology Center. 2014. "Trends and New Directions: Area Agencies on Aging Survey 2014." Accessed December 3, 2015. http://www.n4a.org/publications.

National Care Corps Act of 2015, H.R.2668. 2015. June 4. Accessed February 17, 2016. https://www.congress.gov/bill/114th-congress/house-bill/2668.

National PACE Association. n.d. *Find a PACE Program in Your Neighborhood.* Accessed January 5, 2016. http://www.npaonline.org/pace-you/find-pace-program-your-neighborhood.

National PACE Association, PACE Census and Capitation Rate Information. 2015. Alexandria, VA: National PACE Association.

National Quality Forum. 2015. "Cross-Cutting Challenges Facing Measurement: MAP 2015 Guidance." Accessed February 29, 2016. http://www.qualityforum.org/Publications/2015/03/Cross-Cutting_-Challenges_Facing_Measurement_-_MAP_2015_Guidance.aspx.

National Research Council. 2012. "Aging and the Macroeconomy. Long-Term Implications of an Older Population." National Academies Press. Accessed January 5, 2016. http://www.nap.edu/catalog/13465/aging-and-the-macroeconomy-long-term-implications-of-an-older.

Naylor, M D, K H Bowles, K M McCauley , M C Maccoy, G Maislin, M V Pauly, and R Krakauer. 2013. "High-value transitional care: translation of research into practice." *Journal of Evaluation in Clinical Practice* 19 (5): 727-733.

New York Academy of Medicine. 2009. "Independence at Home Act: A Chronic Care Coordination Program for Medicare That Has Proven Effective in Reducing Costs and Improving Quality for Highest Cost Patients."

Nicholson, N R. 2012. "A Review of Social Isolation: An Important but Underassessed Condition in Older Adults." *Journal of Primary Prevention* 33 (2-3): 137-152.

Office of the National Coordinator for Health Information Technology, Meaningful Use Stage 3, 80 FR 62648. 2015. "2015 Edition Health Information Technology (Health IT) Certification Criteria, 2015 Base Electronic Health Record (EHR) Definition, and ONC Health IT Certification Program Modifications." October 16. Accessed February 17, 2016. https://www.federalregister.gov/-articles/2015/10/16/2015-25597/2015-edition-health-information-technology-health-it-certification-criteria-2015-edition-base.

Older Americans Act of 1965, Public Law 89–73. 1965. Accessed February 29, 2016. http://www.fns.usda.gov/sites/default/files/OAA65.pdf.

Ontario Local Health Integration Network. n.d. *Ontario's LHINs.* Accessed December 7, 2015. http://www.lhins.on.ca/.

Oosting, J. 2014. "Gov. Rick Snyder Pushes to Make Michigan a 'No-Wait State' for In-Home Senior Services." June 2. Accessed October 19, 2015. http://www.mlive.com/lansing-news/index.ssf/2014/06/-snyder_looks_to_make_michigan.html.

Ortman, J M, V A Velkoff, and H Hogan. 2014. "An Aging Nation: The Older Population in the United States." United States Census Bureau. Accessed January 19, 2016. http://www.census.gov/library/publications/2014/demo/-p25-1140.html.

Ostrom, E. 1990. *Governing the Commons: The Evolution of Institutions for Collective Action.* Cambridge, UK: Cambridge University Press.

O'Sullivan, M M, J Brandfield, S S Hoskote, S N Segal, L Chug, A Modrykamien, and E Eden. 2012. "Environmental improvements brought by the legal interventions in the homes of poorly controlled inner-city adult asthmatic patients: a proof-of-concept study." *J Asthma* 49 (9): 911-7.

Ouslander, J G, G Lamb, R Tappen, L Herndon, S Diaz, B A Roos, and A Bonner. 2011. "Interventions to Reduce Hospitalizations from Nursing Homes: Evaluation of the INTERACT II Collaborative Quality Improvement Project." *Journal of the American Geriatrics Society* 59 (4): 754-53.

Ouslander, J, G Lamb, M Perloe, J H Givens, L Kluge, T Rutland, A Atherly, and D Saliba. 2010. "Potentially Avoidable Hospitalizations of Nursing Home Residents: Frequency, Causes, and Cost." *Journal of the American Geriatrics Society* 58 (4): 627–635.

PACE Innovation Act, P.L. 114-85. 2015. November 10. Accessed March 9, 2016. https://www.congress.gov/bill/114th-congress/senate-bill/1362/text/pl.

Parikh, R B, A Montgomery, and J Lynn. 2015. "The Older Americans Act at 50 - Community-Based Care in a Value-Driven Era." *New England Journal of Medicine* 373 (5): 399-401.

Patient Protection and Affordable Care Act, P.L. 111-148. 2010. March 23. Accessed March 4, 2016. https://www.gpo.gov/fdsys/pkg/PLAW-111publ148/pdf/-PLAW-111publ148.pdf.

Pew Research Center. 2014. "Attitudes about Aging: A Global Perspective." Accessed March 1, 2016. http://www.pewglobal.org/2014/01/30/attitudes-about-aging-a-global-perspective/.

PHI National. 2013. "Facts 3: America's Direct Care Workforce." November. Accessed March 25, 2016. http://phinational.org/sites/phinational.org/files/-phi-facts-3.pdf.

Phillips, R S, N S Wenger, J Teno, R K Oye, S Youngner, R Califf, P Layde, N Desbiens, A F Connors, and J Lynn. 1996. "Choices of seriously ill patients about cardiopulmonary resuscitation: Correlates and outcomes. SUPPORT Investigators. Study to Understand Prognoses and Preferences for Outcomes and Risks of Treatments." *American Journal of Medicine* 100 (2): 128-37.

POLST. 2015. *POLST Website.* Accessed October 19, 2015. http://www.polst.org/-about-the-national-polst-paradigm/.

Potts, M K. 1997. "Social Support and Depression among Older Adults Living Alone: The Importance of Friends Within and Outside of a Retirement Community." *Social Work* 42 (4): 348-362.

Qato, D M, J Wilder, L P Schumm, V Gillet, and A C Alexander. 2016. "Changes in Prescription and Over-the-Counter Medication and Dietary Supplement Use

Among Older Adults in the United States, 2005 vs 2011." *JAMA Internal Medicine* 176 (4): 473-482.

Redfoot, D, L Feinberg, and A Houser. 2013. "The Aging of the Baby Boom and the Growing Care Gap: A Look at Future Declines in the Availability of Family Caregivers." Accessed December 3, 2015. http://www.aarp.org/home-family/-caregiving/info-08-2013/the-aging-of-the-baby-boom-and-the-growing-care-gap-AARP-ppi-ltc.html.

Reinhard, S C, L F Feinberg, R Choula, and A Houser. 2015. "Valuing the Invaluable: 2015 Update." AARP Public Policy Institute . Accessed February 15, 2016. http://www.aarp.org/about-aarp/press-center/info-07-2015/family-caregivers-provide-470-billion-in-unpaid-care-aarp-study.html.

Rowland, D. 2013. "What would strengthen Medicaid Long-Term Services and Supports?" Accessed February 11, 2016. https://kaiserfamilyfoundation.-files.wordpress.com/2013/08/drowland_08-01-13-testimony-what-would-strengthen-medicaid-long-term-services-and-supports.pdf.

Scully, T. 2014. "Innovations in Managing Post-Acute Care." Accessed March 1, 2016. http://healthforum.brandeis.edu/meetings/materials/2014-18-march/-naviHealth.Scully.pdf.

Seligman, H K, A F Bolger, D Guzman, A Lopez, and K Bibbins-Domingo. 2014. "Exhaustion Of Food Budgets At Month's End And Hospital Admissions For Hypoglycemia." *Health Affairs* 33 (1): 116-123.

Shell, E. 2013. "The $234 billion job that goes unpaid." Accessed November 13, 2015. http://www.pbs.org/newshour/rundown/the-234-billion-job-that-goes-unpaid/.

Shen, J, R Anderson, R Brook, G Kominski, P S Albert, and N Wenger. 2004. "The Effects of Payment Method on Clinical Decision-Making: Physician Responses to Clinical Scenarios." *Medical Care* 42 (3): 297-302.

Sloane Epidemiology Center at Boston University. 2006. "Patterns of Medication use." Accessed March 1, 2016. http://www.bu.edu/slone/research/-studies/slone-survey/.

Spettell, C M, W S Rawlins, R Krakauer, A Fernandes, M ES Breton, W Gowdy, S Brodeur, M MacCoy, and T A Brennan. 2009. "A Comprehensive Case Management Program to Improve Palliative Care." *Journal of Palliative Medicine* 12 (9): 827-832.

Spillman, B C, J Wolff, V A Freedman, and J D Kasper. 2014. "Informal Caregiving for Older Americans: An Analysis of the 2011 National Study of Caregiving." Accessed November 18, 2015. http://aspe.hhs.gov/report/informal-caregiving-older-americans-analysis-2011-national-health-and-aging-trends-study.

State of Florida Department of Elder Affairs. 2012. "Legislative Report: Long-Term Care Community Diversion Project." Accessed January 19, 2016.

http://elderaffairs.state.fl.us/doea/Evaluation/LTC%20Community%20Diver
sion%20Pilot%20Project%20Report%202011-2012.pdf.

The Care Planning Act of 2015, S.1549. 2015. June 10. Accessed February 17, 2016.
https://www.congress.gov/bill/114th-congress/senate-bill/1549/text.

The Commission on Law and Aging, American Bar Association. 2011. "Giving
Someone a Power of Attorney for Your Health Care: A Guide with Easy-to-
Use, Multi-State Forms for All Adults." Accessed February 11, 2016.
https://www.americanbar.org/content/dam/aba/uncategorized/2011/2011_a
ging_hcdec_univhcpaform.authcheckdam.pdf.

The Dartmouth Atlas of Health Care. 2016. *The Dartmouth Atlas of Health Care.*
Accessed February 16, 2016. http://www.dartmouthatlas.org/.

Thomas, K S, and V Mor. 2013. "Providing More Home-Delivered Meals Is One
Way To Keep Older Adults With Low Care Needs Out Of Nursing Homes."
Health Affairs 32 (10): 1796-1802.

Thomas, K S, and V Mor. 2013. "The Relationship between Older Americans Act
Title III State Expenditures and Prevalence of Low-Care Nursing Home
Residents." *Health Services Research* 48 (3): 1215-1266.

Tinetti, M E, and C Kumar. 2010. "The Patient Who Falls: "It's Always a Trade-
off"." *Journal of the American Medical Association* 303 (3): 258-266.

Tinetti, M E, T R Fried, and C M Boyd. 2012. "Designing Health Care for the Most
Common Chronic Condition—Multimorbidity." *Journal of the American Medical
Association* 307 (23): 2493-2494.

Trout, A T, D F Kallmes, and T J Kaufmann. 2006. "New Fractures after
Vertebroplasty: Adjacent Fractures Occur Significantly Sooner." *American
Journal of Neuroradiology* 27 (1): 217-23.

United States Census Bureau. 2003. "United States Census Bureau, Statistical
Abstract of the United States: 2003, Table No. HS-16. Expectation of Life at
Birth by Race and Sex: 1900 to 2001." Accessed March 29, 2016.
http://www2.census.gov/library/publications/2004/compendia/statab/123ed
/hist/hs-16.pdf.

United States Government Accountability Office, Antipsychotic Drug Use: HHS
Has Initiatives to Reduce Use among Older Adults in Nursing Homes, but
Should Expand Efforts to Other Settings. 2015. United States Government
Accountability Office . Accessed November 23, 2015. http://www.gao.gov/-
products/GAO-15-211.

United States Government Accountability Office, Most Households Approaching
Retirement Have Low Savings. 2015. United States Government Accountability
Office. Accessed December 4, 2015. http://www.gao.gov/products/GAO-15-
419.

United States Government Accountability Office, Older Americans Act: Updated Information on Unmet Need for Services. 2015. United States Government Accountability Office. Accessed January 19, 2016. http://www.gao.gov/products/GAO-15-601R.

Village to Village Network. n.d. *Village to Village Network.* Accessed February 15, 2016. http://www.vtvnetwork.org/.

Voss, R, R Gardner, R Baier, K Butterfield, S Lehrman, and S Gravenstein. 2011. "The Care Transitions Intervention:Translating From Efficacy to Effectiveness." *Archives of Internal Medicine* 171 (14): 1232-1237.

Watkins, L, C Hall, and D Kring. 2012. "Hospital to Home: A Transition Program for Frail Older Adults." *Professional Care Management* 17 (3): 117-23.

West, L A, S Cole, D Goodkind, and W He. 2014. "65+ in the United States: 2010." United States Census Bureau. Accessed January 19, 2016. https://www.census.gov/content/dam/Census/library/publications/2014/demo/p23-212.pdf.

Wieland, D, B Kinosian, E Stallard, and R Boland. 2013. "Does Medicaid Pay More to A Program of All-Inclusive Care for the Elderly (PACE) than for Fee-for-Service Long-Term Care?" *The Journals of Gerontology Series A: Biological and Medical Sciences* 68 (1): 47-55.

Zainulbhai, S, L Goldberg, W Ng, and A Montgomery. 2014. "Assessing Care Integration for Dual-Eligible Beneficiaries: A Review of Quality Measures Chosen by States in the Financial Alignment Initiative." Commonwealth Fund. http://www.commonwealthfund.org/publications/issue-briefs/2014/mar/assessing-care-integration-for-dual-eligible-beneficiaries.

Index